D0897772

STUDIES IN ENGLISH LITERATURE

Volume XXI

TRADITIONAL
IMAGERY OF CHARITY
IN
PIERS PLOWMAN

by

BEN H. SMITH, JR.
Mary Baldwin College

1966
MOUTON & CO.
THE HAGUE · PARIS

Printed in The Netherlands.

TABLE OF CONTENTS

Introduction 7

   I. Lady Holy Church 21

  II. Patience 41

 III. The Tree of Charity 56

 IV. The Good Samaritan 74

  V. Conclusion 94

Bibliography 103

64273

INTRODUCTION

One of the familiar techniques in the historical study of a poem is the examination of its imagery in the light of extra-literary material assumed or proven to be familiar to the poet or his audience, in order to establish the public meanings of the imagery.[1] The ensuing study of some of the imagery of charity in *Piers Plowman* is similar in its approach, in that it relies on the exegetical tradition of the Middle Ages as a key to the meaning and function of selected images of charity in Langland's poem. Before defining the specific procedures of this study, however, one should devote some attention to the general problems associated with the use of the exegetical tradition, since the use of such material as a literary tool has not gone unquestioned among recognized authorities on medieval literature.[2] Accordingly, the ensuing paragraphs will briefly describe the exegetical tradition and the degree to which it has been systematized; they will summarize scholarly opinion for and against the use of the exegetical tradition in literary investigation and will further defend its use; they will cite specific examples of the successful use of exegetical material by competent scholars; and they will suggest reasons for the particular suitability of this approach for *Piers Plowman*.

The exegetical tradition of the Middle Ages theoretically includes all material interpreting biblical texts, thus incorporating

---

[1] For example: John E. Hankins, *Shakespeare's Derived Imagery* (Lawrence, 1955); Rosemund Tuve, *A Reading of George Herbert* (London, 1952).

[2] E. Talbot Donaldson, "Patristic Exegesis: The Opposition", in *Critical Approaches to Medieval Literature*. Selected Papers from the English Institute 1958-1959, ed. Dorothy Bethurum, pp. 1-26.

much religious art, stained-glass, manuscript illumination, many hymns, homilies, and theological tracts incorporating explications of scriptural texts. However, the well-spring of the exegetical tradition, as well as its most comprehensive expression, is to be found in medieval biblical commentary. Biblical commentary, then, as will appear below, is the primary source of scholars seeking to bring the exegetical tradition to bear on medieval literature; in like manner it is the primary source for this study.

Medieval biblical commentary, a vast body of material insufficiently edited, stems from all the religious and ecclesiastical centers in western Europe and spans a period of time stretching from the early Fathers of the Church to the fifteenth century and later. Fortunately, however, a few recent scholars have succeeded in systematizing this unwieldy body of material [3] to the point that its usefulness as a literary tool is considerably enhanced. The work of such scholars, especially of Smalley and Spicq, serves not only to begin the systematization of an unwieldy body of material, but to establish other points which are essential in defending the use of exegetical material in historical criticism. For example, the primary importance of the study of the Bible in the Middle Ages is demonstrated: the fact is established that at least in the later Middle Ages the Bible was read and studied in conjunction with its learned apparatus. Thus, the fourteenth-century reader of the Bible would scarcely have conceived of a scriptural verse in isolation, open to any subjective interpretation which he wished to attach to it. Rather, he would have conceived of it accompanied by all its nexus of traditional interpretation.

However, establishing the fact that the Bible was read in the light of widely-known traditional interpretations does not establish the validity of the use of exegetical material in literary investigation. This question has been under discussion for some time – a discussion which might well be summarized at this point.

---

[3] In particular, Friedrich Stegmüller, *Repertorium Biblicum Medii Aevi* (Madrid, 1940-1955), Vols. II-V; Beryl Smalley, *The Study of the Bible in the Middle Ages* (Oxford, 1952); C. Spicq, *Esquisse d'une histoire de l'exégèse latine au Moyen Âge* (Paris, 1944); Robert E. McNally, *The Bible in the Early Middle Ages* (Westminster, Md., 1959); and Henri de Lubac, *Exégèse médiévale: Les quatres sens de l'Ecriture* (Paris, 1959).

In 1950 D. W. Robertson, Jr., issued a plea for the use of the exegetical tradition in assessing the literature of the Middle Ages.[4] He rightly identifies the use of such material as an aspect of historical criticism, which he defines as "that kind of literary analysis which seeks to reconstruct the intellectual attitudes and the cultural ideals of a period in order to reach a fuller understanding of its literature".[5] Robertson maintains that it is the duty of the serious student not to deplore the intellectual predominance of the Church in the Middle Ages, but rather to examine the ways in which this condition affected the creative activity of the period.[6] Robertson then discusses several examples of Middle English poetry in the light of the exegetical tradition.

E. Talbot Donaldson takes exception to some of Robertson's premises and to the specific applications of some of his theories to literature.[7] With considerable justification Donaldson objects to reducing all of Middle English poetry to the predetermined meaning of an allegory of charity and/or cupidity;[8] he objects to wrenching syntax and the meanings of words in order to force a pre-conceived meaning into a passage,[9] he objects to the inconsistency of reading one line of poetry literally, and the line immediately following metaphorically;[10] he objects to over-loading an obvious symbol with an unnecessary *nexus* of associated meanings.[11] Calling other exegetical critics to task as well, Donaldson objects to burdening a poem with an exegetical interpretation which detracts from the poet's artistic achievement and which rests on a few obscure lines rather than on the overall tenor of the poem.[12] However, no theoretical objections to the use of the exegetical tradition in appraising medieval literature are advanced,

---

[4] "Historical Criticism", in *English Institute Essays* (1950), ed. Alan S. Downer, pp. 3-31.
[5] *Ibid.*, p. 3.
[6] *Ibid.*, p. 4.
[7] See n. 2, above.
[8] *Ibid.*, pp. 2-3.
[9] *Ibid.*, p. 9, for example.
[10] *Ibid.*, p. 11.
[11] *Ibid.*, pp. 15-16.
[12] *Ibid.*, pp. 19-20.

as Donaldson himself admits; [13] instead, he condemns misapplications of the tradition by specific critics. The use of exegetical material in appraising medieval literature is defended both in theory and in practice by R. E. Kaske,[14] and my own defense of the exegetical approach is indebted to him.

Not only are there no valid objections to a proper use of the exegetical tradition in literary investigation, but there is, I think, good reason to utilize it. There can be no question that the Church dominated the intellectual life of the Middle Ages. The central intellectual activity of the medieval churchman for nearly a thousand years was interpreting the Vulgate Bible. Many of the earlier commentaries lived on, either as such or by incorporation into later commentaries; the later commentaries added new interpretations to the available stock, so that the medieval churchman had an ever-increasing fund of meanings, figures, allusions, etc., to draw upon. In discussing any medieval poem from the exegetical point of view, however, one must recognize two further objections: first, that the stock-in-trade of the medieval churchman may not have been the stock-in-trade also of the literary artist; and secondly, that even if it was, exegetical allusion might have had no meaning for the poet's audience. A possible answer offered only tentatively is that even the lay public was probably acquainted with a significant body of exegetical allusion through hymns, sequences, sermons, liturgical offices, and stained-glass. In the specific case of the author of *Piers Plowman*, some sort of ecclesiastical connection has long been granted. But assuming this common stock of allusion available alike to poet and audience, one might still ask whether or not it was a common practice among medieval poets to employ this stock. In reply one can only say that the use of exegetical allusion in Middle English poetry or in particular poems can only be proven by the demonstrable presence of such allusion in the poetry itself.

A number of scholars have already made effective use of exegetical material in dealing with specific Middle English poems.

---

[13]   *Ibid.,* **p.** 1.
[14]   "Patristic Exegesis: The Defense", in *Critical Approaches to Medieval Literature,* **pp.** 27-60.

In the field of Chaucer studies, for example, Father Paul E. Beichner cites a number of pertinent exegetical writings to show that Chaucer's choice of the name Absalom for the clerk of the *Miller's Tale* was purposeful: the biblical Absalom was for the late Middle Ages a type of effeminate male beauty, and his hair typified concupiscent excess, a fact which helps to explain Chaucer's emphasis on Absalom's hair.[15] Robert P. Miller adds a new dimension to Curry's interpretation of the Pardoner, by applying to it the tradition of the scriptural eunuch.[16] Relying on Rupert, Hervé of Bourdieu, the *Glossa*, Bede, Bruno the Carthusian, Peter Lombard, and Hugh of St. Victor among others, he shows how Chaucer's characterization of the Pardoner accords with the exegetical concept of the *eunuchus non dei*, the man sterile in good works. R. E. Kaske uses standard commentary to show how the Summoner's predilection for garlic, leeks, and onions underscores his spiritual depravity.[17] D. W. Robertson, Jr. shows how Chaucer's description of January's garden in the *Merchant's Tale* accords with the exegetical concept of the garden of false delights,[18] and Alfred L. Kellogg shows how the medieval conception of the story of Susannah, related in Dan. xiii, heightens the irony and grotesque carnality of the same tale.[19]

If the exegetical approach has proved fruitful in the "secular" poetry of the layman Chaucer, it has proved even more rewarding in the study of *Piers Plowman,* an explicitly religious poem written by a cleric. Father Dunning uses exegetical writings as well as other material from the Christian tradition in his study of the A-text of *Piers Plowman* [20] and, later, in his study of the B-text.[21]

[15]   "Absalom's Hair", *Medieval Studies,* XII (1950), pp. 222-233.
[16]   "Chaucer's Pardoner, The Sriptural Eunuch, and *The Pardoner's Tale*", *Speculum,* XXX (1955), pp. 180-199.
[17]   "The Summoner's Garleek, Onyons, and eek Lekes", *Modern Language Notes,* LXXIV (1959), pp. 481-484.
[18]   "The Doctrine of Charity in Medieval Literature Gardens", *Speculum,* XXVI (1951), pp. 43-45.
[19]   "Susannah and the Merchant's Tale", *Speculum,* XXXV (1960), pp. 275-279.
[20]   T. P. Dunning, *Piers Plowman: An Interpretation of the A-text* (New York, 1937).
[21]   T. P. Dunning, "The Structure of the B-text of *Piers Plowman*", *Review of English Studies,* VII (1956), pp. 15-237.

Robert W. Frank, Jr., in *Piers Plowman and the Scheme of Salvation*,[22] makes some use of the commentaries of Gregory the Great, St. Augustine, Rabanus Maurus, and Peter Lombard, as well as the *Catena Aurea* and the *Glossa*. E. Talbot Donaldson uses the writings of St. Bernard of Clairvaux and others in his explication of the religious allegory of the C-text.[23] R. E. Kaske shows how Langland combines the tradition of the witnessing elements with the standard interpretation of Ps. xviii, 6, and possibly with elements of the description of the Joachistic third world-age, to make the apparently chaotic speech of Book in Passus XVIII one of the most intellectually controlled in *Piers*.[24] Alfred L. Kellogg uses commentaries on Ps. cxx, 3 to show that the use of *pedem* rather than *sedem* in the Latin following C, II, 111, is a meaningful substitution rather than a scribal error; from commentaries on other psalms, he shows what this substitution brings to its context in a weight of allusion.[25] In the same article Kellogg also shows a pervasive influence of the commentaries on Cant. i,8 and Exodus xv, 1-4 in the account of Lady Meed's ride to Westminster. Finally, in spite of a number of faults, *Piers Plowman and Scriptural Tradition* [26] (further discussed below) by its sheer weight of evidence demonstrates, I believe, the validity of the exegetical approach for *Piers*.

Other Middle English poetry has also been rewardingly examined in the light of exegetical material. For example, Stephen J. Manning uses Rupert, Richard of St. Victor, St. Ambrose, and others to explicate the imagery of the well-known lyric, "I sing of a Myden".[27] There has even been some use of the exegetical approach in the study of Middle English prose: for example, in R. E. Kaske's examination of the leaps of Eve in the Ancrene

---

[22]   *Yale Studies in English*, Vol. CXXXVI (New Haven, 1957).
[23]   *Piers Plowman: The C-text and Its Poet* (New Haven, 1949).
[24]   "The Speech of 'Book' in *Piers Plowman*", *Anglia*, LXXVII (1959), pp. 117-144.
[25]   "Langland and Two Scriptural Texts", *Traditio*, XIV (1958), pp. 385-398.
[26]   By D. W. Robertson, Jr., and Bernard F. Huppé (Princeton, 1951). In this regard, see Kaske's remarks in "Patristic Exegesis: The Defense", *op. cit.*, pp. 32-33.
[27]   "I syng of a Myden", *PMLA*, LXXV (1960), pp. 8-12.

Riwle,[28] Eve's leaps are seen to be ironically projected against the leaps of Christ, as a well-known tradition derived from commentary on Cant. ii, 8. Nor has the use of the exegetical tradition been limited to Middle English literature: G. V. Smithers uses standard exegetical writings in his explication of *The Wanderer* and *The Seafarer*; [29] and Charles S. Singleton uses the writings of Augustine, Gregory, Bede, Abelard, Honorius of Autun, Hugh of St. Victor, Rabanus Maurus, and others in his *Journey to Beatrice*.[30] The exegetical approach has, in fact, been successfully applied to literature outside the realm of the Middle Ages. For example, Rosemund Tuve uses the *Biblia Pauperum,* manuscript illuminations of various kinds, and the *Speculum Humanae Salvationis* in her study of the poetry of Herbert, a study in which she defends her method much as I would defend mine:

I have tried to read many poems, but in the language they were written in, a language of images commonly understood when the poet wrote, believing that the poetry would thus have the beauty and life its creator gave it, but that it would also *thus* translate itself, as all metaphors do, into significances potent here and now.[31]

Thus, exegetical material has been successfully used a number of times in literary analysis, particularly in the realm of medieval literature. Even those medievalists who question the general validity of the exegetical approach have to admit it is theoretically appropriate for the analysis of *Piers*.[32] Indeed, it seems to me that this point must be granted, since *Piers* is an explicitly Christian poem composed by a cleric, and couched in language heavily indebted to Scripture both in allusion and in verbal parallel – an indebtedness whose full extent has, to my knowledge, never been determined, though enough has been demonstrated to make it appear likely that there is a good deal more. And if Smalley and Spicq are correct, with scriptural indebtedness automatically comes exegetical indebtedness.

[28] *Medium Aevum,* XXIX (1960), pp. 22-24.
[29] "The Meaning of *The Seafarer* and *The Wanderer*", *Medium Aevum,* XXVI (1957), pp. 137-153.
[30] *Dante Studies,* Vol. II (Cambridge, Mass., 1958).
[31] *Op. cit.,* p. 22.
[32] Donaldson, "Patristic Exegesis: The Opposition", *op. cit.,* pp. 5-6.

The preceding paragraphs have constituted neither a thorough-going defense of the exegetical approach nor a complete survey of its use. They have served, I hope, both to suggest reasons why the exegetical approach should prove effective in analyzing medieval literature, particularly a poem like *Piers Plowman*, and to point out successful applications of exegetical material to literature. Such successful uses of exegetical material in analyzing literature do constitute a kind of pragmatic defense of the approach, since the final proof of the validity of any literary tool must rest upon its effective use. It is hoped, in fact, that the ensuing discussion of certain traditional figures in *Piers Plowman* will constitute an additional defence of the exegetical approach by further demonstrating its effectiveness. Therefore, the more immediate problems of this specific study should now be considered. In the ensuing paragraphs the primary sources of this study will be described, the choice made among the various texts of *Piers* will be defended, and the reliance of the study on modern scholarship will be discussed briefly. Following this, the expression "traditional imagery of charity" will be defined, the limitations and exact procedures of the study will be discussed, and the final organization will be described.

In the preceding paragraphs, considerable attention was given to the exegetical approach, and it was suggested at one point that the most fruitful source of exegetical material was medieval biblical commentary. However, exactly what commentaries to use in demonstrating the traditional background of Langland's imagery of charity and the relevance of this background for the poem, is largely dictated by practical considerations: that is, the commentaries used are necessarily the ones which are available to me. The most readily available sources are contained in Migne's *Patrologia Latina* [33] (hereafter referred to as "Migne" or as *PL*) which, unhappily, does not extend much beyond the twelfth century – at least 150 years before Langland began writing *Piers Plowman*. Of necessity, I rely on material from the *PL* because of its accessibility. Primarily, however, those pre-thirteenth-cen-

[33] J. P. Migne, *Patrologiae Cursus Completus, Series Latina* (Paris, 1844-1866), 220 volumes.

tury figures are relied on whose works were well-known and extremely influential throughout the course of the Middle Ages: St. Augustine, Rabanus Maurus, Hugh of St. Victor, Honorius of Autun, Peter Lombard, St. Bernard of Clairvaux, Peter of Blois.[34] In addition, Migne's edition of the *Glossa* and of the twelfth-century dictionaries of biblical symbolism are used. The material used from Migne not only falls into the category of the standard commonplace, but it also approaches Langland's period in point of time about as closely as any material printed by Migne (except, of course, for St. Augustine and Rabanus Maurus). Moreover, my use of material somewhat removed from Langland in point of time is not unreasonable, considering the fact that authority, tradition, and convention loom large in medieval exegesis.

However, by far the major debt of this study is to the thirteenth-century commentator, Hugh of St. Cher. His commentary on the whole Bible,[35] basically eclectic, is invaluable as a compendium of commonplaces. Moreover, his was the most widely used commentary of its time; according to Smalley, Hugh's postills "were to be found on the shelves of any self-respecting library in the later middle ages".[36] Hugh's postills were not replaced in the fourteenth century as the standard commentary of the period, and they were still widely used in the fifteenth century.[37] In addition to Hugh, I use the thirteenth-century commentaries of St. Bonaventura, as well as some of his other doctrinal and theological writings.[38]

Unfortunately, few appropriate commentaries of the fourteenth century have been available for use in this study. I have had access to some of the commentary of Nicholas of Lyra, which has been unproductive except as an endorsement of what I had already found to be the received interpretation of a text.[39] It should

[34] Peter of Blois was considered to be a "new Father of the Church" by his twelfth-century contemporaries. Fulbert Cayré, *Manual of Patrology and History of Theology*, trans. H. Howitt (Paris, 1936-1940), II, p. 466.
[35] *Opera Omnia in universum Vetus & Novum Testamentum* (Venice, 1732), 8 vols.
[36] Smalley, p. 270.
[37] *Ibid.*, pp. 271-274.
[38] *Opera Omnia* (Quaracchi, 1882-1902), 10 vols.
[39] According to Smalley, p. 274, when the concern for the Hebrew text

be added that if Father Spicq is correct, the inaccessibility of
fourteenth-century commentary is little cause for regret: "Au-
cune différence réelle ne sépare ce siècle [XIVe] du précédent
au point de vue exégétique; L'esprit et la methode des travaux
scripturaires se retrouvent identiques dans les commentaires de
1200 à 1400." [40] Moreover, to mitigate the deficiency in the use
of fourteenth-century commentary, I use the carefully conventional exegesis of Denis the Carthusian (1402-1473).[41] Such a
process of bracketing the century in question seems to be the best
procedure to follow until fourteenth-century commentary is made
available to the modern student.

Though biblical commentary constitutes the major portion of
the source material for this study, other exegetical material, when
pertinent, is included. In addition, material from the Christian
tradition which is not strictly exegetical, but which proved highly
relevant for *Piers Plowman*, is occasionally included. Therefore,
references are made from time to time to stained-glass, manuscript illuminations, theological *Summae* and doctrinal treatises,
homiletic material, and the liturgy. This apparent inconsistency
results from the empirical nature of this study; when research
was begun on a given image, it was by no means certain where it
would lead; and to exclude relevant material on the grounds that
it is not strictly exegetical would be, I think, a false consistency.
In any case, by far the greater dependence of the study is on biblical commentary.

The B version of *Piers Plowman* was chosen for study because
it is fuller than the A version, and because it is more familiar,
more often studied, and in the consensus of learned opinion a
better poem than the C version. My own research has revealed
nothing to contradict this generally held opinion about the supe-
riority of the B version. A comparison of the imagery in the B
and C versions is, of course, beyond the scope of this study. I am

---

and the rabbinical tradition is extracted from Nicholas' commentaries, only
the most conventional allegorizations remain.

[40]   P. 331.

[41]   *Opera Omnia* (Montreuil, 1896-1913), Vols. I-XIV. For Denis' conven-
tionality, see Cayré, *op. cit.*, II, p. 708.

convinced, nevertheless, that where the imagery of charity in the C version differs significantly from that of the B version, the latter is characterized by greater intellectuality and aesthetic excellence. The primary importance of the C version for this study is as an occasional gloss on the B version.

Skeat's text of the B version,[42] hereafter referred to as the B-text, is used, since it is the only readily available text of the B version. The possible inaccuracy of Skeat's edition must concern all students who undertake research in *Piers Plowman*. I grant the difficulty, admitting that a critical text of the poem might affect my reading in a few instances. I urge the mitigating circumstance, however, that research in *Piers Plowman* can ill afford to await the advent of a critical text of all the versions of the poem. Moreover, though the best procedure generally is to establish a text before interpreting it, there are instances in which it is useful to have a convincing interpretation of a passage at hand when attempting to establish its text. That convincing interpretations are necessary in establishing the text of *Piers* follows from Kane's discussion of the difficulties besetting the editor of the A-text.[43] For various reasons discussed at length by Kane – reasons which apply equally well to the manuscripts of the three different versions of the poem – the manuscripts of the A version do not yield to the established techniques of textual criticism. The genealogical relationships of the various manuscripts can not be determined, nor can the degree of authority of a given manuscript be determined by any other means. Therefore, the variants themselves are the only source of textual authority: that is, a presumption of originality is established by determining the variant most likely to have given rise to the other variants. The reading of the text thus arrived at is credible only if it is grammatically and syntactically sound *and if it can be supported by a convincing interpretation*. Moreover, though a few of my findings will rest on a close reading of the text, unless Skeat was grossly inaccurate – as we

---

[42] Walter W. Skeat, ed., *The Vision of William Concerning Piers the Plowman by William Langland* (Oxford, 1886).
[43] George Kane, *Piers Plowman: The A Version* (London, 1960), pp. 53-149.

have no reason to suspect – the main lines of my argument should stand. For the most part I deal with series of images which are undergirded by discernible patterns – images, that is, which have interrelated traditional overtones and consistency of function. Minor textual variations, then, should have no material effect. It might be added that changes in the received opinion regarding the authorship of *Piers* will not materially affect this study. Certain imagery of the B version, a self-contained and extremely popular medieval poem, is studied in the light of its traditional background. No analysis is offered of artistic or poetic development from one version to another, nor are any biographical implications drawn. Even if some configuration in B is derived from the imagery of A plus interpolations by someone other than the author of A, the configuration, I think, still would have existed for this artistic interpolator, and presumably for his reader, as an integral whole. That is, however many hands are at work in B, the shaper of the final form of any given passage was functioning as a poet, or else the B version is beneath the notice of the ever-increasing group of critics who are proclaiming its artistic excellencies. In short, by keeping my eye on the configurations themselves as they were widely read and presumably widely appreciated in the Middle Ages, I have avoided, I hope, the whole question of authors and interpolators.

Besides Skeat's texts and notes there has been little reliance in this study on modern scholarship, since the territory covered is relatively unexplored. Such reliance, in fact, is limited for the most part to accounts of stained-glass and of manuscript illuminations. However, in connection with the use made of modern scholarship a word should be said about Robertson and Huppé's *Piers Plowman and Scriptural Tradition*, the only major scholarly work apparently impinging on the field of this study. The ensuing study and Robertson and Huppé's book differ in aim, scope, and method. The aim of Robertson and Huppé is to explicate the "thought structure" of *Piers* by placing it in its traditional milieu; my aim is to explicate specific imagery of *Piers* by placing it in its traditional milieu. Robertson and Huppé's scope includes the whole poem, passus by passus; my scope is limited to relative-

ly short passages from four passus. Robertson and Huppé's method, for better or for worse, is to look for patterns in the poem
which they have assumed from the outset; my method is to examine the details of certain passages to see what patterns, if any,
emerge. Because of such far-reaching differences in aim, method,
and scope, there is practically no duplication in the two studies;
and the few instances of overlapping will be obvious from my
references in the text and in the notes.

Having considered at some length the primary and secondary
sources for this study, let us indicate what is meant by "traditional imagery of charity", and then go on to describe the procedure and the limitations of the study.

The question, "What is poetic imagery?" is a difficult one indeed and would not be raised fruitfully here. Suffice it to say that
in this study the term *imagery* is used in its broadest sense to refer
to concrete language which, in context, has a primarily non-
literal function. For example, the word *tree* is concrete and is obviously capable of a wide range of literal applications. However,
in Passus XVI, when Langland describes the tree of charity, he is
of course using this concrete term in a non-literal sense. As for
"traditional imagery", it is concrete but non-literal poetic language readily available to the poet from some source other than
his own imagination – in this case, from the Christian tradition.

The procedure for research can be summarized as follows. If
a particular image suggests a specific scriptural reference, one
would of course proceed immediately to commentaries on the
passage in question. For example, the use of the figure of the
Good Samaritan in Passus XVIII would naturally send one to
the commentaries on Luke x, 30-35.[44] In many instances, however,
a scriptural reference is not suggested. In such cases one would
consult the medieval dictionaries and compendia of biblical sym-
bols printed by Migne and by Pitra.[45] Failing this, one would
resort to a concordance, though such a procedure can be burden-
some, especially if the key word has several synonyms. Once a

[44]   All scriptural citations are from the Vulgate Bible or the Douay translation.
[45]   J. B. Pitra, *Spicilegium Solesmense* (Paris, 1852-1858).

possible scriptural reference has been determined, one would examine commentaries on the pertinent passage and on related texts, since medieval exegetes, seldom thinking of scriptural verses in isolation, normally cite a number of related passages from both the Old and the New Testaments. However, the implication should not be drawn from the above that every image discussed below is derived primarily from Scripture, and that the commentaries are used only to establish public meanings. Many images based ultimately on Scripture are derived primarily from the exegetical tradition itself. For example, in Passus I the image of love as the treacle of heaven is derived from commentaries on Numbers xxi, though there is no mention of treacle in the scriptural source, but only in the commentary.

The limitations of the ensuing discussion of the imagery of charity are pragmatic. That is, if the inductive procedure described above yielded significant results for a given image, then these results are discussed in one of the chapters which follow. If not, then the image is given short shrift or not discussed at all. One should not conclude, however, that the study is over-selective, since the majority of images are discussed and those sections of *Piers Plowman* where the charity imagery is concentrated are emphasized.

The basic organization of the study is local, with the emphasis on those four sections of the poem where the charity imagery is concentrated: Lady Holy Church's speech (Passus I); Patience's discussion of the lives of Dowel, Dobet, and Dobest (Passus XIII); Anima's discussion of charity (Passus XV-XVI); and Will's encounter with the Good Samaritan (Passus XVIII). If the study carries conviction, it will not only help to revivify the imagery of charity in these areas of concentration; it will also serve as a further pragmatic defense of the exegetical approach, and will further the work of placing a significant poem in the dominant tradition of which it partakes, the medieval Christian tradition.

I

LADY HOLY CHURCH

The first extensive use of figurative language in connection with
charity in *Piers Plowman* occurs in Passus I, 11. 146-162:

> For trewthe telleth that loue . is triacle of heuene;
> May no synne be on him sene . that vseth that spice,
> And alle his werkes he wrou3te . with loue as him liste;
> And lered it Moises for the leuest thing . and moste like
>   to heuene,
> And also the plente of pees . moste precious of vertues.
>   For heuene my3the nou3te holden it . it was so heuy of
>   hym-self,
> Tyl it hadde of the erthe . yeten his fylle,
>   And whan it haued of this folde . flesshe and blode taken,
> Was neuere leef vpon lynde . li3ter ther-after,
> And portatyf and persant . as the poynt of a nedle,
> That my3te non armure it lette . ne none hei3 walles.
>   For-thi is loue leder . of the lordes folke of heuene,
> And a mene, as the maire is . bitwene the kyng and the
>   commune;
> Ri3t so is loue a ledere . and the lawe shapeth,
> Vpon man for his mysdedes . the merciment he taxeth.
> And for to knowe it kyndely . it comseth bi myght,
> And in the herte, there is the heude . and the hei3 welle.

According to Lady Holy Church, truth, knowledge of God,
teaches that love is "treacle of heaven". The modern connotations of *treacle*, sticky sweetness, must not divert the reader. Skeat
glosses the word as a healing medicine, and in a note to the line
in question further defines it as "an antidote against poisons
containing flesh of vipers".[1] The *OED* validates this definition,

[1]   Vol. II, p. 27.

defining a *triacle* specifically as an antidote in the form of a salve, effective against venomous bites.

The image of love as the "treacle of heaven" is based on the standard interpretations of two related scriptural passages. In Num. xxi, 8-9 is an account of how the Hebrew Children, wandering in the desert, were plagued with serpents because of their murmurings against God. After they repented, Moses was told by God to make a brazen serpent and to set it up on a forked prop as a sign before the people. Thereafter, when anyone was struck by a serpent, he could be saved by looking on the brazen serpent. In John iii, 14, this incident is applied to Christ: "Et sicut Moyses exaltavit serpentem in deserto, ita exaltari oportet Filium hominis." Following the example of the evangelist, biblical commentators made the brazen serpent an Old Testament type of Christ. For example, both Rabanus Maurus and Denis the Carthusian call the brazen serpent a type of the Saviour, who overcame the venom of Satan, the ancient serpent.[2] The connection between the brazen serpent and Langland's image is even more apparent from Hugh of St. Cher on John iii, 14. After citing the relevant passage from Numbers, Hugh goes on to say:

Christus dicitur serpens: quia sicut de serpente fit venenum, et de serpente fit tyriaca in veneni remedium: ita facto de veneno serpente, i. de diabolo, voluit Dominus fieri serpens, ut de eo fieret tyriaca contra venenum diaboli. Et hoc est, quod Exod. 7 serpens Moysi devoravit serpentes Magorum. Item serpens aeneus non est vere serpens, nec venenum habet, et ideo significat Christum, qui habuit similitudinem carnis peccatricis, non carnem peccatricem. Habuit quidem veram carnem, sed non vere peccatricem, imo peccatrice similem, ut dicitur Rom. 8 Deus filium suum misit in similitudinem

---

[2] *PL.* 108, 713: "Sed quid illud significat, quod morsus mortiferi serpentium, exaltato et respecto aereo serpente, sanabantur, nisi quod nunc in typo Salvatoris, qui ferum antiquumque serpentem in patibulo triumphavit, diaboli venena superantur, ita ut qui vere expresseque imaginem Filii Dei passionemque ejus conspexerit, conservetur?" Vol. XIV, p. 42b: "Praterea Deus per serpentem aeneum sic voluit subvenire, ad praefigurandum mysterium passionis redemptionisque Christi. Ideo ait Glossa: non serpens aeneus sanavit illos, sed sacramentum mysterii, id est mors Christi in serpente praefigurata. Christus quippe antiquum serpentum triumphavit in cruce, et ejus venenum devicit: ut qui vere imaginem Christi et ejus passionem conspexerit, salvetur."

carnis peccati, et de peccato damnavit peccatum, i. per tyriacam
venenum expulit, et de Christo, qui vocatur peccatum pro similitudine,
damnavit diabolum, qui peccatum dicitur veritate, et origine, i., valde
peccator, et origo peccati.[3]

Here the connection between the brazen serpent and Langland's
image becomes explicit in Hugh's word *tyriaca*, which is the Latin
equivalent of ME *triacle*, as well as the parent of the English
form.[4]

Since the brazen serpent hanging on a prop before the people
was conventionally interpreted as a prefiguration of the Passion
(above, note 2), it seems that Langland is describing love in terms
of its supreme manifestation, Christ's suffering; or, more generally, it seems that this charity figure is endowed by the exegetical
tradition with strong overtones of the supreme manifestation of
charity, Christ. Literally, "May no synne be on him sone . that
veeth that spice", means either that the *spice* of love removes the
stain of sin, or that that *kind* (*species*) of remedy removes the
stain of sin. If the latter meaning is the intended one, then the
overtones of the Passion carry over into this line: the "treacle"
of Christ's Passion removes the stain of original sin. On the other
hand, if Langland is comparing love to a spice, he has some precedent in the exegetical tradition. For example, in commenting on
Cant., i, 11, "While the king was at his repose, my spikenard
sent forth the odor thereof", Hugh of St. Cher glosses "spikenard" as both charity and humility.[5] However, the predominant
exegetical associations of spices are with penitence, mortification

---

[3] Vol. VI, fol. 297ᵛ.
[4] The image of the treacle of heaven appears elsewhere in English in
Caxton's *Royal Book* (S.T.C. 21429), chap. cxli: "The serpent of brasse
that henge on the perche, sygnefyeth the body of Jhesu Cryst hangying on
the crosse. That was the serpent withoute venym of whyche was made the
tryacle of our sauvacyon for who somever feleth hym smyton and en-
venymed of prykying and styngyng with the venemous serpentes of helle
that ben the deuylles late hym beholde by veray fayth on the serpent of
brasse. That is to say that he haue in his hert parfyte mynde of the passyon
of Jhesu Cryst and anone he shal be heled and delyuerd of the temptacyons
of the enemye that is the deuyll."
[5] Vol. III, fol 110ᵛ; Honorius of Autun, in commenting on Cant. I, 11-
13, connects *spice* with Christ (*PL*. 172, 376-378).

of the flesh, good works, the virtuous life, and the gifts of the Holy Ghost.[6]

The lines, "And alle his workes he wrouȝte . with loue as him liste; / And lered it Moises for the leuest thing . and most like to heuene", pose a minor syntactic problem. The antecedent of *he* is indefinite, and it is not clear whether Moses "learned" or "taught" the importance of love. However, a reference to God's creative acts seems likely, and the allusion to the transmission of the law, summarized in the New Testament as love for God and for one's neighbor, is apparent. In any event, the statement is literal, not figurative.

The *plente of pees* of line 150 is identified by Robertson and Huppé as a Christ figure, though they do not document their statement.[7] Further investigation of the point has failed to reveal the plant of peace as a commonplace figure for either Christ or charity. Christ as the Prince of Peace or simply as *Pax* is, of course, a great commonplace; and Christ is often enough compared to a tree or to a vine.[8] One should not discount the possibility, I think, that a fusion of these two concepts occurred in Langland's own imagination. Whatever its source, the relevancy of a figure of a plant will become apparent when the lines immediately following are placed in their traditional context.[9]

This passage, containing an extended figure, reads:

> For heuene myȝte nouȝste holden it . it was so heuy of hym-
> self,
> Tyl it hadde of the erthe . yeten his fylle,
> And what it haued of this folde . flesshe and blode taken,
> Was neuere leef vpon lynde . liȝter ther-after,

---

[6] See, for example: *PL.* 113, 1144 on Cant. iii, 6; *PL.* 210, 711 on Cant. iii, 6 and iv, 16; *PL.* 112, 866 on Cant. iv, 10, 16; *PL.* 172, 402 on Cant. iii, 6; *PL.* 183, 993-994 on Cant. i, 12; *PL,* 184, 192 on Cant. iv, 14; and Hugh of St. Cher, Vol. III, fol. 121r on Cant. iii, 6 and iv, 6 and fol. 125v on Cant. iv, 10.

[7] P. 46.

[8] For example, *PL.* 172, 383; *PL.* 210, 837.

[9] The possibility of pun on *plant* and *plenty* should not be overlooked. The expression *abundantia pacis* is frequently found in conjunction with the figure of the dew on the fleece of Gedeon (see discussion below). This traditional association stems from Ps. lxxi, 6-7.

And portatyf and persant . as the poynt of a nedle,
That myȝte non armure it lette . ne none heiȝ walles.

(I. 151–156)

In this passage, implicit associations with Christ already noted in connection with the treacle of heaven become explicit in the reference to the Incarnation: "Tyl it hadde of the erthe . yeten his fylle, / And whan it haued of this folde . flesshe and blode taken." On this basis the passage will be considered primarily as a configuration of images traditionally associated with Christ, the supreme manifestation of charity.

Several scriptural passages with their glosses lie behind this figure of heavenly love falling to earth and becoming incarnate. One of these is Is. xlv, 8: "Rorate caeli desuper, et nubes pluant Justum: aperiatur terra, et germinet Salvatorem: et justitia oriatur simul: ego Dominus creavi eum." The standard commentaries clarify the connection of this passage with the Incarnation. For example, Hugh of St. Cher says:

Rorate coeli desuper. Hic orat Ecclesia adventum filii, qui solo rore coelestis gratiae non operatione naturae, quasi furtim descendit in alvum Virginis. . . . Aperiatur terra, idest Beata Virgo per consensum cordis, non per fractionem corporis. Et germinet Salvatorem, idest, Christum, qui salvum fecit populum suum a peccatis eorum.[10]

In Isaiah the dew drops down from heaven, the clouds rain down the just one, and the earth opens and buds forth a saviour; in Langland heavenly love falls from heaven and eats of the earth to become fully incarnate. In addition, the passage from Isaiah accords with the preceding figure in Langland of a plant, the plant of peace. This parallelism, plus the traditional connection of the scriptural passage with the Incarnation, increases the likelihood that Isaiah xlv, 8, with its commentary, lies behind Langland's figure.

Another relevant passage is from one of the prophetic psalms, Ps. lxxi: "Descendet sicut pluvia in vellus: et sicut stillicidia stillantia super terram" (verse 6). Hugh, connecting this passage with the Incarnation, glosses the fleece as the virginity of Mary,

10   Vol. IV, fol. 102ᵛ.

the ground as her humility, and the rain as deity or grace. The
fleece is appropriate, not only because it is immune to carnal lusts
– having been removed from the body – but also because "Ex
vellere isto facta est a Spiritu Sanctu vestis filii Dei, idest, caro.
. . . Erat autem tunica ejus inconsutilis. Nos habemus tunicas con-
futas expartibus, scilicet, a patre, et matre: sed Christus tantum
a matre." [11] The commentators inevitably connect Ps. lxxi, 6 with
the story of the fleece of Gedeon, related in Judges vi, 36-40.
Gedeon, appointed by God to deliver Israel from the Midianites,
prays for a sign. He will spread a fleece out on the ground, and
if the dew falls on the fleece only, while the surrounding area is
dry, then Gedeon will know that he is truly called to save Israel.
In the morning the fleece is wet with dew, while the ground is dry.
The fleece is a type of the Virgin Mary; the dry ground, of the
rest of womankind.[12] The entire figure of the dew falling on the
fleece was often taken as a prefiguration of the Incarnation. St.
Bonaventura uses the figure in a Nativity sermon.[13] In a window
at Lyon it is used in connection with the Nativity,[14] and St.
Bernard of Clairvaux calls it a clear prefiguration of the virgin
birth.[15] In the *Speculum Humanae Salvationis* the fleece of Gedeon
is one of the three Old Testament types of the Conception:

> De qua vellere fecit sibi tunicam cristus vera sophia
> Concepcio marie signum nostre erat redempcionis
> Vellus igitur gedeonis est benedicta virgo maria
> Qui vestiri voluit tunica nostre humanitatis
> Vt nos vestiret stola perpetue iocunditatis.[16]

[11]   Vol. II, vol. 181v.
[12]   Denis the Carthusian, Vol. III, p. 150b: "Iterum, per hoc vellus intelligitur gloriosissima Virgo Maria; per aream, ceterarum universitas femina-
rum. Itaque Virgo Deifera primo prae ceteris impleta est omni rore divino-
rum charismatum, in tantum quod materna fecunditas virginalisque puristas
convenerunt in ea, a qua praerogativa ceterae omnes feminae siccae fue-
runt: quibus vel materna fecunditati, aut aliis donis gratiose perfusis, prae-
stantissima Virgo ab omni virilis seminis contagione, omnique concupiscen-
tiaruum humore mansit siccissima."
[13]   *Opera Omnia* (Quaracchi, 1882-1902), Vol. IX, p. 127a.
[14]   Émile Mâle, *Religious Art in France in the Thirteenth Century,* trans.
Dora Nussey (New York, 1913), p. 38.
[15]   *Super Missus Est Homilia II: PL.* 183, 64.
[16]   Jean Philippe Berjeau, ed., Facsimile Edition (London, 1861), fol. 20r,
col. 2, 11.3-7.

The figure of the fleece of Gedeon, with its associated scriptural allusions, looms large in the liturgy of Advent, the time of preparation for the great act of the Incarnation. For example, during Vespers for the second Sunday in Advent, Is. xlv. 8 ("Rorate . . . Salvatorem") is followed by the antiphon, "Orietur sicut sol Salvator mundi: et descendet in uterum virginis sicut imber super gramen. Alleluia." [17] During the third Sunday in Advent, the response is used: "Descendet Dominus sicut pluvia in vellus. Orietur in diebus ejus justitia, Et abundantia pacis." [18] The following is an antiphon for lauds the Saturday before the fourth Sunday in Advent: "Expectetur sicut pluvia eloquium Domini: et descendet sicut ros super nos Deus noster." [19] Such examples, which could easily be multiplied, demonstrate the familiarity in the Middle Ages of the fleece of Gedeon and its related figures as images of the Incarnation.

The specific figure of the dew on the fleece of Gedeon is such a medieval commonplace [20] that it probably underlies Langland's figure directly. Such a probability is augmented by the equation made both by Hugh of St. Cher and in the *Speculum Humanae Salvationis*, for example, between the fleece and Christ's "clothing", the flesh and blood of His human nature. When Langland says, "And whan it haued of this folde . flesshe and blode taken", *folde* has a primary meaning of "earth". However, *folde* can just as easily mean "a piece of cloth". Langland's awareness of the traditional comparison between the flesh and blood of the Incarnation with human vesture is established, for example, in Passus V, line 495: "And sith with thi self sone . in owre sute deydest."

This configuration of heavenly love falling to earth can be still further clarified by the commentaries. According to Langland, heaven could not hold charity, or Christ. In his commentary on

[17] Francis Proctor and Christopher Wordsworth, eds., *Breviarium Ad Usum Insignis Ecclesiae Sarum* (Cambridge, 1882), Vol. I, lxxxi.
[18] *Ibid.*, cvii.
[19] *Ibid.*, cxxix.
[20] See, for example, F. J. E. Raby, *A History of Christian-Latin Poetry from the Beginning to the Close of the Middle Ages* (Oxford, 1927), pp. 371-373; and Yrjo Hirn, *The Sacred Shrine* (London, 1912), pp. 306-312.

Is. lxiv, 1, "Utinam dirumperes caelos, et descenderes", Hugh of St. Cher says that in His love of mankind, and in the impetuosity of His desire to become incarnate, the Son of God rent the heavens asunder; that the gate of heaven was too narrow to permit the outpouring of so much grace, so that the walls of heaven had to be broken down.[21]

The detail that love was "heuy of hym-self" could evolve from details such as those above from Hugh, where divine love precipitously wishes to be fulfilled in the Incarnation; or it could reflect a metaphysical concept discernible in the Christian tradition at least as early as St. Augustine. In the *City of God* St. Augustine, having mentioned the sensual love which suffices the nature of beasts and the love of growth and fruitfulness which fulfills the nature of plants, alludes to the natural desire of the elements for their due places: that is, in ascending order, earth, water, air and fire. He concludes: "Nam velut amores corporum momenta sunt ponderum, sive deorsum gravitate, sive sursum levitate nitantur. Ita enim corpus pondere, sicut animus amore fertur, quocumque fertur." [22] A similar idea is developed in the *Confessions*:

Requies nostra, locus noster. Amor illuc attollit nos, et Spiritus tuus bonus exaltat humilitatem nostram de partis mortis (Psal. ix.15). In bona voluntate pax nobis est (Luc. ii.14). Corpus pondere suo nititur ad locum suum. Pondus non ad ima tantum est, sed ad locum suum. Ignis sursum tendit, deorsum lapis. Ponderibus suis aguntur, loca sua petunt. Oleum infra aquam fusum, supra aquam attollitur; aqua supra oleum fusa, infra oleum demergitur; ponderibus suis aguntur, loca sua petunt. Minus ordinata, inquieta sunt: ordinantur et quescunt. Pondus meum amor meus; eo feror quecumque feror.[23]

---

[21]   Vol. IV, fol. 161r: "Item per diruptionem intelligitur violentia, et praecipitatio, sive impetuositas facti tanta enim charitate, et dilectione Filius Dei voluit incarnari, et tam subito, et quasi insperato fecit, ut victus, et coactus charitate coelos dirupisse dicatur, et quasi infamis factus ad miserias nostras subito descendisse. ... Item affluentiam gratiae coelestis ad nos emanandam ostendit Propheta per verbum disruptionis, dicens: Utinam dirumperes coelos, et descenderes, q.d. Janus brevis est, nisi rumpatur murus coeli ad exitum tantae gratiae, et tam copiose defluentis, *Gen.* vii: Rupti sunt omnes fontes abyssi magnae, et cataractae coeli apertae sunt."
[22]   Book XI, chap. xxviii: *PL.* 41, 342.
[23]   Bk. XIII, chap. ix: *PL.* 32, 848.

The basic principle may be summed up: as weight is to the body, so love is to the soul. Such a principle is reiterated by Hugh of St. Cher [24] and by St. Bonaventura.[25]

Using the C-text as a gloss on the B-text, one finds that there is another traditional detail underlying the figure of love's heaviness and, indeed, the basic figure of love falling to the earth and becoming incarnate. In C.II. 150-151, it is stated that heaven could not hold love because it seemed so heavy until it had poured itself out on the earth. Such a pouring forth of love goes back to Phil. ii, 5-7. "Hoc enim sentite in vobis, quod et in Christo Iesu; / Qui cum in forma Dei esset, non rapinam arbitratus est esse se aequalem Deo; / Sed semetipsum exinanivit formam servi accipions, in similitudinem hominum factus, et habitu inventus ut homo." The reference to the Incarnation is explicit.

Configurations closely related to that of the fall of heavenly love from heaven to earth occur elsewhere in *Piers*. Also in Passus I and separated from the passage under consideration by no more than thirty lines is a description of the revolt in heaven. The description of the consequent expulsion from heaven of Satan and his legions parallels that of the fall of charity:

> Lucifer with legiounes . lerned it obedience in houene,
> But for he brake buxumnesse . his blisse gan he tyne,
> And fel from that felawship . in a fendes liknes,
> In-to a depe derke helle . to dwelle there for cure;
> And mo thowsandes with him . than man couthe noumbre,
> Lopen out with Lucifer . in lothelich forme,
> For thei leueden vpon hym . that lyed in this manere:
>   *Ponam pedem in aquilone, et similis ero altissimo.*
> And all that hoped it miȝte be so . none heuene miȝte hem
>   holde,
> But fellen out in fendes liknesse . nyne dayes togideres,
> Til god of his goodnesse . gan stable und stynte,
> And garte the heuene to stokye . and stonden in quiete.

(I. 111–21)

That these lines are to be connected with the passage which, a few lines later, describes the fall of heavenly love seems apparent

[24] Vol. VII, fol. 263r.
[25] Vol. III, pp. 639a, 806b.

from line 118-119: "None heuene miȝte hem holde, / But fellen out in fendes liknesse." In this instance, the fall from heaven is an image *in malo*, suggesting the antithesis of the incarnation of charity.

Related to both of these passages is a configuration of images from Passus XII. Imagination is distinguishing between *scientia* and *sapientia* when he says:

> For the heihe holigoste . heuene shal to-cleue,
> And loue shal lepe out after . in-to this lowe erthe,
> And clennesse shal cacchen it . and clerkes shullen it fynde;
> *Pastores loquebantur ad inuicem.* (XII, 141–143)

The basic image is that of the leaps of Christ, a medieval commonplace resting ultimately on Cant. ii, 8.[26] And, parenthetically, the image of the "leaps" *in malo* may be used in the description in Passus I of the expulsion of Satan and his legions from heaven:

> And mo thowsandes with him . than man couthe noumbre,
> Lopen out with Lucifer . in lothelich forme.
> (I, 115–116)

While the basic imagery is that of Christ's "leaps", however, in Passus XII material traditionally associated with Christ, specifically the Incarnation, is used as a figure of charity, as is the case in Passus I. Moreover, Imagination is discussing *sapientia* while Lady Holy Church is relating what truth teaches about love; and, for that matter, before the expulsion from heaven Satan is taught *trouthe* by the Trinity, but he ignores it (I, 108-112). Thus a clear organic relationship can be seen to exist between the three configurations.

The second half of the configuration originally under consideration involves the idea that after love was incarnate, it became light ("portable") and piercing as the point of a needle, so that no armor or high walls could hinder it. Luke xviii, 25 reads: "Facilius est enim camelum per foramen acus transire, quam divitem intrare in regnum Dei." The *acus*, "needle", of this pas-

[26] For an account of the tradition of the leaps of Christ, see R. E. Kaske, "Eve's 'Leaps' in the *Ancrone Riwle*", *Medium Aevum*, XXIX (1960), pp. 22-24.

sage has traditional associations with the double nature of Christ.
Commenting on this scriptural passage, Hugh of St. Cher says:

Item acus est Christus, ut dicit Chr[ysostom] Rectus ut acus, cujus
prima pars subtilis est, et acuta, non perforata, sed perforans, et significat Divinitatem, quae impassibilis est, posterior pars grossa est, et
perforata et significat humanitatem, quae passa est. Haec acus reser-
civit tunicam nostrae immortalitatis, quae in Adam acissa fuerat per
peccatum, et dirupta. Haec acus consuit carnem spiritui, et Judaicum
populum gentili, et ruptam amicitiam Angelorum, et hominum copu-
lavit.[27]

This passage explains the metaphorical "piercing" attributed by
Langland to charity. Love "pierces" in repairing or joining together, just as a needle literally pierces cloth being repaired or
joined together. Through love the tunic of human immortality
was restored; through love flesh is stitched to spirit, Jew to Gen-
tile, angel to angel, and man to man.

According to Langland, when love had become incarnate (i.e.,
after the fulfillment of the Incarnation), neither armor nor high
walls could restrain it. In view of the centrality of the Christ-
figure in the whole passage, the primary allusion here may well
be to Christ's resurrection from the tomb guarded by the Roman
soldiers. However, this image is weighted with other traditional
associations. For example, a passage from the psalms emphasizes
the destruction of armor by God: "Venito, et videte opera Domini, quae posuit prodigia super terram: / auferens bella usqui
ad finem terrae. Arcum conteret, et confringet arma: scuta com-
buret igni" (xlv, 9-10). Hugh makes the following comment on
this passage:

Scuta autem sunt defensiones peccatorum. ... Sunt autem defen-
sionees peccatorum quatuor, scilicet exsusatio, verecundia, diminutio,
comparatio. Hoc scutum quadrangulum ponit Diabolus circa collum
ficte confitentis. ... Scuta combussit igni divini amoris, docens nos
non solum peccata, sed etiam bona nostra accusare.[28]

Here the significant detail, as far as the passage from Langland

---

[27]   Vol. VI, fol. 241v.
[28]   Vol. II, fol. 121v.

is concerned, is that the shield composed of four specious defences
for sin is destroyed by the fire of divine love.

The connection between sin and armor also looms large in
Hugh's commentary on Ezechiel. For example, he compares some
of the ramifications of sin to a veritable armory: a buckler to
obstinacy in sin; a lance to the habit of sin; a bow to spitefulness
of heart; an arrow to levity of discourse; a staff to the perpetra-
tion of evil works; a pike to the corruption of a bad example.[29] In
Ezech. xxxviii, 3-4, the armor and military resources of Gog are
listed. Hugh comments on this passage at some length:

Et nota quod isti equites, i. Demones dicuntur vestiti loricis, idest,
malis, et multis hominibus fortibus. Fortes enim hujus mundi per ini-
quitatem colligati fiunt lorica ad defensionem Diaboli, vel peccati. . . .
Vel loricae quibus armantur equites Diaboli, idest homines mali qui
impugnant mores Ecclesiae, sunt peccatorum connexiones. Ita enim
connectunt peccata peccatis, quod jaculum verbi divini non potest eos
penetrare, et salubriter vulnerare. Sicut enim in lorica una macula
tenet aliam: ita in congerie peccatorum una culpa tenet, et roborat
aliam. . . . Et sic una macula connectitur alteri in lorica peccati. . . .
Per scutum obstinationem, vel peccati excusationem; . . . et nota de
scuto, quod quamdiu stat, repellit jacula; sed dum cadit, cito frangitur,
in casu enim debile. Ita est de excusatoribus peccatorum: quamdiu
vivunt, ad repellenda jacula verbi divini fortes sunt, et infrangibiles;
sed in casu, idest in morte divinae animadversioni non possunt resis-
tare.[30]

In this commentary the armor of sin is drawn up against the spear
of the divine word in a way which closely parallels the armor
which, in Langland, would hinder the "piercing" of divine love.
In the Christian tradition, then, armor glossed *in malo* involves
some immediate aspect of sin; in Langland's context, *armure* is
probably a metonymy for sin.

In addition to armor, according to Langland no walls can hinder the "piercing" of love. Like armor, the wall has traditional
associations with sin. The relevant scriptural passage is Cant. ii,
9: "En ipso stat post parietem nostrum respiciens per fenestras
. . ." According to the *Glossa, paries* is the condition of mortality

which we have erected by sinning.[31] According to Honorius of Autun, *paries* is original sin separating us from God:

Paries est murus, qui domum a domo separat, et significat originale peccatum vel mortalitatem quae de peccato venit, nos a Deo separat. Quem murum coepit Adam aedificare, et omnis posteritas ejus laborat eum consummare. . . . Post hunc murum Christus stetit, ut eum impelleret, quia mortalis est factus, ut originale peccatum destrueret.[32]

Hugh of St. Cher, as is often the case, makes an even more revealing comment. The wall which the bridegoom, Christ, stands behind, is threefold – a fact which could easily explain Langland's use of the plural, *walles*. One is the wall of human nature, askew rather than upright since the fall. A second is the wall made of heaped-up sin and cemented by carnal affections, which, however, can be *pierced* and even destroyed by penitence. The third is the wall made up of the difficulties and cares of this life which divert our full attention from God. The salient detail for Langland's image follows: "Stat igitur *dilectus* post hunc triplicem parietem paratus adjuvare *volentes penetrare, vel diruere, vel transgredi parietes istos*" [my italics].[33] The force of the image of the armor and high walls, then, is that the powers of sin and darkness are ineffectual in hindering charity. In addition, the armor overcome by divine love most certainly foreshadows the great Christ-knight configuration of Passus XVIII.

Close analysis of the details of the configuration being considered does not account for the underlying paradox. The weight of unembodied charity is such that charity becomes incarnate; whereupon charity becomes as light as a linden leaf. In other words, unembodied love was heavy; after it took on body, it became light. I doubt that one can explain the creative process whereby this effective paradox was realized. However, several comments are worth making in this connection. In the first place, in the Middle Ages the Incarnation was keenly felt as paradox: an event resulting in both the virgin-mother and in the god-man. Thus it is fitting for paradox to be employed in a poetic context

[31]   *PL.* 113, 1129.
[32]   *PL.* 172, 390-391.
[33]   Vol. III, fol. 117v.

where the basic figure is one of the Incarnation. Secondly, Langland's paradox reflects another Christian paradox: before the fullness of divine love could be diffused over mankind, it had to be encompassed within the flesh of one man. Charity had to assume human flesh to overcome the walls and armor of evil on man's behalf. Langland's use of paradox, then, is not out of keeping with the Christian tradition or with the medieval temper of mind. For example, the incarnate heaviness and subsequent lightness of charity is paralleled to a considerable degree in the liturgy for St. Stephen's day, December 26. The basic figure underlying the first lectio is that on the preceding day Christ put on the robe of mortality while today Stephen put off the corruptible for the incorruptible. The third lectio states: "Charitas ergo quae ad terram de caelo deposuit Christum, ipsa Stephanum de terris elevavit ad caelum." The remaining readings are devoted predominantly to a consideration of charity.[34] Such observations, of course, do not fully explain Langland's paradox; they do, I think, illumine the paradox and place it in its traditional context.

A summary of Langland's figurative treatment of charity thus far considered follows. The fall of love from heaven and its subsequent incarnation followed by the penetration of the armor and high walls seems to be an overt, climactic reference to the earthly career of Christ as it is related in the New Testament. The earlier allusions to the *treacle,* to the creative acts, and to Moses emphasize the connection between Christ's earthly career and various events related in the Old Testament. In addition, there is some justification for seeing the succeeding lines in *Piers* as containing allusions to the career of Christ after his earthly ministry had been completed.

The poet continues, "For-thi is loue leder . of the lordes folke of heuene": because love ate of the fold of earth in order to overcome the armor and walls of evil, love is foremost of the people of the lord of heaven. Certain traditional associations for the line result in the progression from Incarnation to subdual of the armor and walls of evil to leading the lord of heaven's people. For example, there is an inherent parallel between the passage from

[34] *Sarum Breviary,* cxcix-ccv.

Langland thus far considered and Eph. iv, 8-10: "Ascendens in altum *captivam duxit captivitatem*: dedit dona hominibus. Quod autem ascendit, quid est, nisi quia et descendit primum in inferiores partes terrae? Qui descendit, ipse est et qui ascendit super omnes coelos, ut impleret omnia [my italics]." The descent here referred to is conventionally associated, not only with the descent into limbo, but also with the Incarnation, while the ascent leading captivity captive is usually connected with the freeing of the souls of the just from limbo after the harrowing of hell.[35] Hugh of St. Cher's comment on the passage states that Christ ascended in order to lead his own (*suos*) into heaven.[36] Elsewhere Hugh speaks of Christ's victorious ascent from the lower regions, riding on a cloud and borne on angel wings, after he had *destroyed the wall between and made both one*.[37] Thus, when the line being considered is placed in its poetic context and its traditional overtones are noted, probable overtones of the harrowing of hell emerge, and *walles* of the preceding line may take on an additional significance of the walls of hell. A number of other passages from *Piers* relate to the interpretation of this line. For example, this passage, combining imagery of the Incarnation with specific references to Eph. iv, 8, the harrowing of hell, and, in this case, "blowing" the lord's folk into paradise, is found in Passus V:

> And sith with thi self sone . in owre sute deydest
> On godefryday for mannes sake . at ful tyme of the daye,
> There thi-self ne thi sone . no sorew in deyth feledest;
> But in owre secte was the sorwe . and thi sone it ladde,
>> *Captiuam duxit captiuitatem.*
> The sonne for sorwe ther-of . les syʒte for a tyme
> Aboute mydday whan most liʒte is . and mele tyme of seintes;
> Feddest with thi fresche blode . owre forfadres in derknesse,
> *Populus qui ambulabat in tenebris, vidit lucem magnam;*
> And thorw the liʒte that lepe oute of the . Lucifer was blent,
> And blewe alle thi blissed . in-to the blisse of paradise.
>> (V, 495–503)

Note also line 498, "But in owre secte was the sorwe . and thi sone it *ladde*."

---

[35] For example, Denis the Carthusian, Vol. XIII, p. 313b.
[36] Vol. VII, fol. 174r.
[37] Vol. V, fol. 47r.

Returning to the passage in the first passus, one should note
that the term *leader,* repeated in line 159, shifts the imagery into
a political framework, most obviously indicated by the word
maire. To continue with the text:

> And a mene, as the maire is . bitwene the kyng and
>   commune;
> Riȝt so is loue a ledere . and lawe shapeth,
> Vpon man for his mysdedes . the merciment he taxeth.

Love, like the town mayor, not only leads the people, but also
mediates between them and the king; love also judges and punishes. While the modern mind may have difficulty seeing love as
mediator, law-shaper, and judge, the medieval mind would certainly not. Love brings accord and reconciliation; the imperatives to
love God and one's neighbor are the reshaping under the new dispensation of the old Mosaic law; finally, in terms of medieval
Christianity, judgment and punishment must always be executed
ex caritate.[38] Thus Lady Holy Church conveys to Will further
attributes of love by means of a politically framed configuration.
However, without derogating the obvious importance of this political framework, one should also point out that mediation,
"shaping" the law, and judgment are all important traditional
aspects of Christ's involvement with mankind. Christ as a
"mean" or mediator is a great commonplace based directly on
scripture: for example, "Filioli mei, haec scribo vobis, ut non
peccetis. Sed et si quis peccaverit, advocatum habemus apud Pa-
trem, Iesum Christum iustum", (I John ii, 1); or, "Unde et sal-
vare in perpetuum potest accedentes per semetipsum ad Deum;
semper vivens ad interpellandum pro nobis" (Heb. vii, 25). And
the commentators, of course, picked up this scriptural commonplace. For example, just as Langland speaks of love as a mediator between the king and the common people, Hugh of St. Cher
speaks of Christ as the mediator between God and man and between one man and another.[39] Much earlier, St. Augustine, like

---

[38]   See, for example, *PL.* 44, 236. In this connection it might also be noted
that according to the inscription on hell-gate in the *Divine Comedy,* love
is one of the founding forces of hell (*Inf.* iii, 6).

[39]   Vol. VII, fol. 156r.

Langland, had conflated the functions of leading and mediating. He observes that Satan, the mediator of death, leads men to death through pride, while Christ, the meditor of life, leads man to life through humility.[40] Christ, of course, also shapes the law – the New Law of love. Or to put it another way, He reshapes the Old Law given on Mt. Sinai. And the point that Christ's final role in human affairs is that of judge does not require elaboration. Does it not seem probable then, that at this point in *Piers* one finds a basically political configuration re-enforced by material traditionally associated with Christ – material that would serve to unify this configuration with the imagery that precedes it?

Lady Holy Church's characterization of love continues:

> And for to knowe it kyndely . it comseth bi might,
> And in the herte, there is the heuede . and the hei3 welle.
>
> (I, 161–162)

These lines can be rendered, "And, to recognize it properly, love begins in power, and in the heart is the source and deep fount of love." The latter image, that of the heart as the source and fount of love, requires no explanation. It was an image as familiar in the Middle Ages as it is today. For example, "Medium quippe est cor hominis, inde fons amoris erumpit." [41] However, the notion that love originates in might does perhaps require some comment. It should be recalled that might or power is conventionally the primary attribute of God the Father. Langland's point seems to be that it is the Father, the source of all things, who gives mankind the natural ability to experience *caritas*. Moreover, the point becomes explicit in the next two lines:

> For in kynde knowynge in herte . there a my3te bigynneth
> And that falleth to the fader . that formed vs alle.
>
> (I, 163–164)

Having told Will the source of love, Lady Holy Church draws this part of her description of charity to a close with an extended allusion to God's greatest act of charity, His self-sacrifice:

[40]   *De Trinitate,* Bk. IV, chap. x: *PL.* 42, 896-897.
[41]   Pseudo-Hugh of St. Victor, *De Fructibus Carnis et Spiritus, PL.* 176, 1005.

And that falleth to the fader . that formed vs alle;
Loked on vs with loue . and lete his sone deye
Mekely for owre mysdedes . to amende vs alle;
And ʒet wolde he hem no woo . that wrouʒte hym that peyne,
But mekelich with mouthe . mercy he bisouʒte
To haue pite of that poeple . that peyned hym to deth.

(I, 164–169)

Beginning with line 170, Lady Holy Church exhorts Will to human acts of charity in a lengthy passage which is not as a whole germane to this study. However, the meaning of one figure of charity in this passage is considerably heightened when it is placed in its traditional context. Lines 183-187 read:

For James the gentil . jugged in his bokes,
That faith with-oute the faite . is riʒte no thinge worthi,
And as ded as a dore-tre . but if the dedes folwe;
Fides sine operibus mortua est, &c.
For-thi chastite with-oute charite . worth cheyned in helle;
It is as lewed as a laumpe . that no liʒte is inne.

Why is chastity without charity compared to a lamp without a light? Why will chastity without charity be chained in hell? And what is the connection with faith without works? These questions are answered in commentaries on Matt. xxv, 1-12, the parable of the wise and the foolish virgins. According to this parable, when they went forth to meet the bridegroom, the five wise virgins took oil with their lamps, but the five foolish virgins took only their lamps without a supply of oil. While they were awaiting the bridegroom, they slept; but when the cry arose at midnight that he was approaching, they awakened. However, the foolish virgins had no oil for their lamps, and they had to hurry away to procure a further supply. While they were gone, the bridegroom arrived and took the five wise virgins with him into the marriage feast. When the five foolish virgins returned, they found the door already closed; and when they begged for admittance, the bridegroom said that he did not know them. According to Hugh of St. Cher the lamps represent works, "quae secundum continentiam fiunt". The oil, however, is identified with charity, "quae est

super omnes virtutes sicut oleum superenatat".[42] Applying this
interpretation to the passage in question, the works of continence
(lamps) without charity (light-producing oil) will be damned,
just as the foolish virgins were denied entrance to the marriage
feast. Langland's figure of the lamp without a light rather than
the lamp without oil suggests a conflation of a commonplace figure of charity, fire, with the conventional interpretation of the
parable. Moreover, Hugh further equates the lamps with faith
and the oil with works, which equation accounts for the applica-
bility of Langland's figure to the text from James. Along the same
lines, Denis the Carthusian points out, with a bit of false etymol-
ogizing, that the name *lampas* signifies faith and works.[43] Thus,
Langland's figure of the lamp without a light becomes a metonymy
for the five foolish virgins. Furthermore, Langland's use of the
figure in a context concerned with the necessity of charitable
works in addition to faith, is in complete accordance with the
traditional associations of the figure.

Thus Lady Holy Church's speech falls into two basic parts.
From line 146 through line 168 she describes and characterizes
the abstract quality of charity by means of a series of highly
allusive yet concrete images derived primarily from the Christian
tradition and weighted by traditional associations with Christ.
Charity is the healing salve for the sickness of sin; it motivates
the creative processes; it is the summation of all law; it is the only
source of peace. It contracted into a span of human flesh in order
that it might diffuse itself over the whole creation and destroy
the walls and armor of evil. Love leads mankind to God; love also
mediates between mankind and God. Love acts as judge and dis-
ciplinarian. The ability to know this virtue is naturally implanted
by God in man's heart, the deep fount of love. In the second part
of her speech, line 173 through line 201, Lady Holy Church
asserts the individual's obligation to manifest in his daily life the
virtue of charity. In this part of her speech, the figurative language is neither as concentrated nor as complex, though there is
effective use of a configuration derived from the parable of the

---

[42]   Vol. VI, fol. 77v.
[43]   Vol. XI, p. 271a.

wise and the foolish virgins. Most appropriately, the *effictio caritatis*, constructed of imagery fraught with traditional associations with Christ, is joined to the *exhortatio* by Lady Holy Church's command to emulate Christ's supreme manifestation of charity in His human life:

> Here myȝtow see ensamples . in hym-selue one,
> That he was miȝstful and meke . and mercy gan graunte
> To hem that hongen him an heiȝ . and his herte thirled.
> For-thi I rede ȝow riche . haueth reuthe of the pouere.
>
> (I, 170–173)

Finally, in a summarizing statement, Lady Holy Church returns to the theme underlying the image of the treacle – the healing properties of charity – a theme which may look forward to the healing powers of the Good Samaritan as he personifies charity in Passus XVII. In this final passage Lady Holy Church asserts that charity gives access to eternal life, and then she concludes by reiterating the opening statement of her discourse on charity:

> Loue is leche of lyf . and nexte owre lorde selue,
> And also the graith gate . that goth in-to heuene;
> For-thi I sey as I seide . ere by the textis,
> Whan alle tresores ben ytryed . treuthe is the beste.
>
> (I, 202–205)

II

PATIENCE

After Lady Holy Church's comprehensive delineation, the further
consideration of charity is conspicuously absent from the *visio*.
In fact, it is not until Passus XV, well into the *vita,* that Anima,
at Will's request, discourses at length on the nature of charity
(ll. 145-339). However, Patience's description of Dowel, Dobet,
and Dobest in Passus XIII evolves into a brief discussion of various manifestations of the spirit of charity with a concomitant use
of traditional figures. For this reason, a consideration of this passage is included. Passus XIII, lines 135-156, reads:

> "At ȝowre preyere", quod Pacyence tho . "so no man displese
> hym;
> *Disce,*" quod, he, "*doce . dilige inimicos.*
> *Disce,* and Dowel . *doce,* and Dobet;
> *Dilige,* and Dobest . thus tauȝte me ones
> A lemman that I loued . Loue was hir name.
> 'With wordes and with werkes,' quod she . 'and wille of thyne
> herte,
> Thow loue lelly thi soule . al thi lyf-tyme;
> And so thow lere the to louye . for the lordes loue of heuene,
> Thine enemye in al wyse . euene-forth with thi-selue.
> Cast coles on his hed . and al kynde speche,
> Bothe with werkes and with wordes . fonde his loue to wynne;
> And lay on hym thus with loue . til he laughe on the;
> And but he bowe for this betyng . blynde mote he worthe!
> Ac for to fare thus with thi frende . foly it were,
> For he that loueth the lelly . lyte of thyne coueiteth.
> Kynde loue coueiteth nouȝte . no catel but speche,
> With half a laumpe lyne in latyne . *ex vi transicionis.'*
> I bere ther in a bouste . Dowel ybound
> In a signe of the Saterday . that sette firste the kalendare,

And al the witte of the Wednesday . of the nexte wyke after;
The myddel of the mone . is the miȝte of bothe.
And here-with am I welcome . there I haue it with me." [1]

This passage, especially its latter part, has continued to baffle students of *Piers*, though scholars like Skeat and Goodridge have offered pertinent suggestions as to its underlying meaning.[2]

In lines 136-139, Patience proposes for the lives of Dowel, Dobet, and Dobest, the progression *disce, doce, dilige inimicos,* identifying *disce* and Dowel, *doce* and Dobet, and *dilige inimicos* and Dobest.[3] In the next few lines, Patience, quoting his lemman, love, seems to apply this or a similar progression specifically to the spiritual growth of the individual Christian:

"With wordes and with werkes", quod she . "and wille of thyne
    herte,
Thow loue lelly thi soule . al thi lyf-tyme;
And so thow lere the to louye . for the lordes loue of heuene,
Thine enemye in al wyse . euene-forth with thi-selue".

(XIII, 140–143)

The individual is enjoined to love his own soul, which, in turn, will teach him to love his enemy.[4] The repetition of the progression is elliptical, but is to be implied, I think, from the phrase "lere the". *Lere* could, of course, mean *learn* in the fourteenth century. However, the *OED* makes it clear that the older meaning of *teach* was in current usage well past the fourteenth century. Patience's statement, then, might be paraphrased: "By learning to love your own soul, teach yourself to love your enemies."

The concept upon which Patience is relying in the second pro-

---

[1] From Skeat's edition with the exception of line 152, which is quoted by permission of E. Talbot Donaldson from the forthcoming Athlone Press edition of the B-text.
[2] Skeat, Vol. II, pp. 196-197; J. F. Goodridge, trans., *Piers Plowman by William Langland* (Baltimore, 1959), pp. 304-308.
[3] A general consideration of the lives of Dowel, Dobet, and Dobest is obviously beyond the limits of this study. It is worth noting, however, that Langland's equation between love of enemies and Dobest is traditional. Hugh of St. Cher says of *Diligits inimicos vestros:* "Loquitur hic Dominus perfectis" (Vol. VI, fol. 167ʳ).
[4] The ensuing interpretation is based on the assumption that *so* in line 142 means "thus", rather than "so long as"; the latter is the meaning of *so* in line 135.

gression is derived from the Christian tradition. It will be recalled that it is not only the Christian's duty to love God, but also to love God's image in his fellows.[5] Furthermore, the Christian is enjoined to love God's image in his enemies. For example: *"Diligite inimicos vestros*, quantum ad id quod habent a Deo, puta naturam ad Dei imaginem factam, et beatitudinis susceptivam."[6] Or: "Debemus ergo inimicos propter Deum diligere, quoniam ipso hoc jussit, atque ad ejus imaginem sunt plasmati."[7] In the latter instance, note the similarity between *propter Deum* and "for the lordes loue of heuene" (XIII, 142). Moreover, such an inclusive love for mankind was thought to incorporate a proper love of one's self. Indeed, the New Testament summary of the Law implies a proper love of self in commanding that the Christian love his neighbor *as himself*; and the idea is elaborated in an anonymous *Tractatus de charitate*: "Non enim potest quis proximum suum diligere, sicut semetipsum, nisi diligat se ipsum."[8]

Certain mystics of the twelfth century, writing on charity, incorporate these traditional concepts into a description of a *distensio charitatis*. For example, the *Tractatus De Charitate* equates love of self with the "sabbath of the seventh day"; love of neighbor with the "sabbath of the seventh year" (Lev. xxv, 4); and love of God with the "sabbath of sabbaths". It then goes on to describe the progression from love of self to love of one's neighbor,[9] paralleling a portion of Patience's statement. Significantly,

---

[5] Hugh of St. Cher, Vol. VII, fol. 354ʳ: "Frater enim tuus imago Dei est, si ergo non diligis imaginem Dei, nec eum cujus est imago, diligis: ergo mendax es si te Deum diligere dicis, et fratrem odis." Denis the Carthusian, Vol. II, p. 258a: *"Non oderis fratrem tuum in corde tuo.* Ex hoc arguitur, quia secundum legis intentionem omnis proximus, in quantum rationalis creatura ad Dei imaginem facta, et beatitudinis capax, sit ex caritate amandus."

[6] Denis the Carthusian, Vol. XI, p. 74a.

[7] *Ibid.*, Vol. II, p. 259a.

[8] *PL.* 184, 610. See also Peter Lombard, *PL.* 192, 813.

[9] *Ibid.:* "Sane, si ab hoc puriore thalamo cordis, quod primo sabbato [dilectio sui ipsius] dedicavit, migraverit ad illud diversorius, ubi solet gaudere cum gaudentibus; coinfirmari infirmis, scandalizatis couri, suamque senserit animan fratribus suis indissolubili glutino charitatis unitam, adeo ut nec suscipio sinistra, nec invidiae motus, nec aestus iracundiae aut tristitiae, possit aliqua occasione surripere."

there follows a description of the *distensio charitatis* to include
one's enemies. In a tract by Peter of Blois, closely related to the
tract cited above (see *PL*. 184, 583-584), there appears the same
description of the distension of charity.[10] A similar description
appears in the *Speculum Charitatis* of Aelred of Rievaulx; here
the author rhapsodizes on the peace and tranquility of the soul
which has proceeded from love of self to love of all mankind including enemies.[11] It would seem, then, that a concept of the *distensio charitatis* underlies Patience's speech: a concept similar to
the one underlying certain mystical tracts on charity. However,
the correlation is not exact. The threefold progression described
in the tracts on charity moves from love of self to love of all mankind, including enemies, to love of God. This final stage is not
explicit in what Patience says. However, it is to be taken for
granted in any medieval discussion of charity, and its omission at
this point emphasizes the moral rather than the theological aspect
of charity.

A figure traditionally connected with charity occurs in conjunction with the distension of charity to include one's enemies:

> Cast coles on his hed . and al kynde speche,
> Bothe with werkes and with wordes . fonde his loue to wynne.
>
> (XIII, 144–145)

This figure of the burning coals is specifically identified with
charity by Goodridge.[12] He correctly relates the image to Prov.
xxv, 21-22: "Si esurierit inimicus tuus, ciba illum: si sitierit, da
ei aquam bibere: / prunas enim congregabis super caput eius, et
Dominus reddet tibi"; and to its echo in Rom. xii, 20: "Sed si

---

[10] *De Charitate Dei et Proximi, PL.* 207, 911-912.
[11] *PL.* 195, 581: "Vere tempus pacis, tempus quietis, tempus tranquillita-
tis, tempus gloriae et exsultationis. Quid enim molestiae, quod perturba-
tionis; quid moeroris, quod anxietatis ejus poterit interpolare laetitiam, qui
a primo illo Sabbato [dilectio sui ipsuis], in quo laborum suorum fructibus
pascitur, ad humus divinae similitudinis statum gratia pleniore progreditur,
ut omne hominum genus uno mentis amore complectens, nullius injuris
moveatur; sed, sicut indulgentissimus aliquis pater ergo charissimum sibi
filium phrenesi laborantem, ita ille erga suos afficiatur inimicos, ut quo
magis ab eis injuriatur, eo profundiori charitatis affectu inferentibus sibi
molestiam compatiatur?"
[12] P. 304.

esurierit inimicus tuus, ciba illum: si sitit, potum da illi; hoc enim faciens, carbones ignis congeres super caput ejus." The commentaries attest to Goodridge's identification. The conventional nature of the image is demonstrated by the fact that Alanus de Insulis identifies the burning coals of both scriptural passages as charity.[13] Denis the Carthusian makes the same identification and includes the idea of conquering or overcoming one's enemies with charity, thus echoing "And but he bowe for this betyng" (XIII, 147).[14]

The lines immediately following suggest that the Christian is not called upon to manifest his love for his friends in the same way that he is for his enemies:

Ac for to fare thus with thi frende . foly it were,
For he that loueth the lelly . lyte of thyne coueiteth.
(XIII, 148–149)

Then the cryptic description of "kynde loue" follows:

Kynde loue coueiteth nou3te . no catel but speche,
With half a laumpe lyne in latyne . ex xi transicionis.
(XIII, 150–151)

I believe that an understanding of the almost unintelligible "half a laumpe lyne in latyne ex vi transicionis" is central to any interpretation of this passage. Commenting on this line a number of

[13] Distinctiones, PL. 210, 731: "Carbo, proprie, est charitas; unde Paulus: Hoc faciens, carbones ignis congeres super caput ejus, id est patientia tua accendens eum in charitate divnia." PL. 210, 914: "Pruna ... Dicitur charitas, unde Salomon, Et prunas congregabis super caput ejus, id est ad charitatem mutabis."
[14] Vol. VII, p. 160b: "Si esurierit inimicus tuus, ciba illum; si sitierit, da ei aquam, id est aptum poculum, bibere: id est, redde ei bona pro malis, ut beneficiis vincas eum. Ideo subditur: prunas enim, id est caritatis fomenta et incentiva, congregabis super caput ejus, id est in corde ipsium, inducento eum ad considerationem caritatis, pietatis, et beneficentiae tuae: ex quibus cor ejus rancorem abjaciet, et tuo accendetur amore. Sic enim vincitur malum in bono." In addition, there are any number of exegetical passages where burning coals are glossed as charity, or at least as burning with the fire of charity. For example: PL. 112, 888; PL. 183, 743; Hugh of St. Cher, Vol. I, fol. 29v; Vol. II, fol. 34r; Vol. IV, fol. 304v St. Bonaventura, Vol. IX, p. 342.

years ago, Henry Bradley called attention to a specifically grammatical application of the Latin noun *transitio*.[15] The Lewis and
Short dictionary gives a definition similar to Bradley's: "In
gram., *an inflection* by declension or conjugation." In the Middle
Ages, however, grammatical transitivity was not such a simple
matter. An apt illustration comes from the *Grammatica Speculativa* attributed to Duns Scotus:

And we should know that the two differences, transitive and intransitive, are taken metaphorically in constructions, i.e. by a certain
similitude of real transitivity. For some one is said really to be transitive (*transire*) when he crosses (*transit*) from one place to another
different from the first. When however some one proceeds to some
first term, remaining in it and not turning aside, then he is said not
to be transitive. So in the intransitive construction; because the dependence of one, i.e., of the second constructibile, goes to the first,
and stays there, it is accordingly called intransitive. e.g., "Socrates
runs". But in a transitive construction the dependence of the second
does not go to the first but crosses to something different from the
first. Accordingly it is deservedly called transitive.

We should note further that in the intransitive construction the
second constructibile, which depends upon the first, strives to be identified with it in some respect. But in the transitive construction the
second constructibile does not depend upon the first, but in its dependence recedes from the first and strives to be diversified from it
in some respect. Hence it is that ancient grammarians in giving defini-
tions of the transitive and intransitive construction, gave them by
"the same" and "different", saying that an intransitive construction
is one in which the constructibilia pertain or seem to pertain as it
were to the same; a transitive construction however is one in which
the constructibilia pertain to what are different or seem to pertain
to what are different.

That however should be understood according as was said; because
the constructibilia in an intransitive construction are said to pertain
to the same, in so far as the second, which by its mode of signifying
depends upon the first, strives to be identified with it in some respect.
Moreover, constructibilia in a transitive construction are said to pertain to what are different in so far as the second constructibile, which
is its dependence recedes from the first constructibile, strives to be
diversified from it in some respect.[16]

---

[15] "Some Cruces in Piers Plowman", *MLR*, V (1910), pp. 340-342.
[16] *On the Modes of Signifying: A Speculative Grammar*, trans. Charles
Glenn Wallis (Ann Arbor, 1938), p. 49. The Latin reads: "Et sciendum,

It is probable, then, that in the expression *ex vi transicionis* Langland is invoking a principle of grammatical transitivity such as the one described above: a principle whereby the *constructibilia* of "half a lamp line in Latin" pertain to different things rather than to the same thing; Langland's Latin phrase might be translated: "By the power, or by the principle, of grammatical transitivity." Such a suggestion has initially one possible weakness. The complete phrase *ex vi transicionis* may have had a grammatical meaning which does not coincide precisely with the meaning to be evolved from a translation of the component parts of the phrase.[17] But even if this should be so, it would not be unlike Langland's method to alter occasionally the familiar interpretation of

---

quod istae duae differentiae, transitivum et intransitivum, sumuntur in constructionibus metaphorice, id est, per quamdam similitudinem *transitus realis*. Nam aliquis dicitur realiter *transire*, quando transit *de uno loco ad alium a primo diversum*. Cum autem quis procedit ad aliquem terminum primum, et *in isto manet*, inde non divertens, tunc dicitur *non transire*. Sic in constructione *intransitiva*, quia dependentia unius, id est, posterioris constructibilis, vadit ad primum, inde *non* transiens, ideo *intransitiva* dicitur, ut: Socrates currit; in constructione vero *transitiva* dependentia posterioris non vadit ad primum, sed transit ad aliud diversum a primo, ideo *transitiva* merito nuncupatur.

Notandum ulterius, quod in constructione *intransitiva* posterius constructibile, dependens ad primum, aliquo modo nititur identificari cum eo. In constructione autem *transivita* posterius constructibile non dependet ad primum, sed per suam dependentiam a primo recedens, aliquo modo nititur diversificari ab eo. Et inde est, quod antiqui Grammatici dantes definitiones constructionis *transitivae*, et *intransitivae*, dabant eas per *idem*, et *diversum*, dicentes. Constructionem *intransitivam* esse illam, in qua constructibilia pertinent ad idem, vel tanquam ad idem videntur pertinere; *constructionem* autem *transitivam* esse illam, in qua constructibilia pertinent ad *diversa*, vel videntur pertinere ad diversa.

Illud autem debet intelligi modo, quo dictum est; quia pro tanto constructibilia in constructione *intransitiva* dicuntur pertinere ad idem, quia posterius constructible, per suum modum significandi, dependens ad primam, aliquo modo nititur identificari cum eo. Pro tanto etiam constructibilia in constructione *transitiva* dicuntur pertinere ad diversa, quia posterius constructibile, per suam dependentiam a primo constructibili recedens, aliquo modo nititur diversificari cum eo, vel ab eo." (John Duns Scotus, *Grammaticae Speculativae*, Quaracchi ed., Florence, 1902, pp. 153-155).

[17] Professor R. E. Kaske has discovered the entire phrase in certain twelfth-century commentaries on Priscian. See " *'Ex Vi Transicionis'* and its Passage in *Piers Plowman*", *JEGP*, Vol. LXII (1963), pp. 32-60.

traditional material; in the immediately preceding line, in fact, he seems to be re-shaping an old adage.[18]

Various medieval theologians and exegetes, especially St. Bonaventura,[19] employ the concept of grammatical transitivity. Hugh of St. Cher invokes the aspect specifically described in the *Grammatica Speculativa*: that is, that in an intransitive construction the components pertain to different things. For example, commenting on Eph. ii, 14, Hugh says: "*In Medium parietem maceriae*. Intransitiva est constructio, idest, parietem, qui est maceria.*"* [20] Again, on Cant. iii, 6: "*Ex aromatibus myrrhae, et thursis* intransitive, hoc est, ex myrrha, et thure, quae sunt aromata." [21] Most significant of all is Hugh's comment on Ps. iv, 7, "Signatum est super nos lumen vultus tui Domine: dedisti laetitiam in corde meo":

Lumen vultus tui, idest, luminosus vultus tuus, idest ratio. . . . Vultus Dei dicitur ratio, quia sicut per vultum homo homini assimilatur, et homo cognoscit hominem, ita per rationem similes sumus Deo, et Deum cognoscimus. Vel potest legi *transitive* [my italics] sic: Vultus Dei dicitur ratio: Lumen hujus vultus, est gratia, quia sicut moneta est informis, donec imago Regis ei per cuneum imprimatur, ita ratio nostra deformis est, donec per gratiam Dei illustretur. Ratio enim est imago creationis: sed gratia Dei est imago recreationis.[22]

Hugh thus glosses a portion of this verse both *transitively* and *intransitively*. Intransitively, "thy light-giving countenance" is equated with the reason. Transitively, "countenance" and "light" refer to different things: "countenance" is equated with reason; "light", with grace. Reason is connected with the image of God stamped on His created world; grace, with the image of God stamped on His re-created world.[23]

---

[18] *OED,* II, 1108: *Covet,* le, example 1: "Sene it is in ald sawe, þat kynde coueyts ay his lawe." (St. Cuthbert, ca. 1450).

[19] Vol. I, pp. 104a, 115a, 116a, 445b-446a, 650a; Vol. II, p. 36b.

[20] Vol. VII, fol. 171ʳ.

[21] Vol. III, fol. 121ʳ.

[22] Vol. II, fol. 9ᵛ.

[23] Cf. Peter Lombard, *Commentarium in Psalmos* (*PL.* 191, 88): "Lumen est lumen gratiae tuae, quo reformatur imago tua in nobis, qua tibi similes sumus. . . . Vultus ergo Dei, ratio nostra accipitur. . . . Haec autem ratio per peccatum hominis deformata est . . .; sed per gratiam Christi reformata

It is possible, in fact, that Ps. iv, 7 may be precisely what Langland is referring to by his "half a laumpe lyne in latyne . *ex vi transicionis*". "Half-line" is a piece of nomenclature peculiarly fitted to the psalms, since in the liturgy each verse was chanted antiphonally. *Lumen*, a light, can also refer to a source of light or a lamp.[24] Thus Langland's "Latin half-line containing a reference to a lamp" (as I would render it), becomes the first half of Psalm iv, verse 7: "Signatum est super nos lumen vultus tui Domine." This "half line", with both a *transitive* and an *intransitive* interpretation is, *ex vi transicionis*, to be associated by Langland's reader with its *transitive* interpretation. Thereby *vultus* is to be equated with *ratio*, the image of God stamped on the creation; and *lumen* with *gratia*, the image of God stamped on His new creation. There are many other biblical verses containing references to *lumen*, a light or a lamp. However, the particular lamp-line here proposed is by no means an obscure one. For example, it is one of the texts used by Hugh of St. Victor in his *Miscellanea*.[25] It is the opening text of the sermon "De Inventione Sanctae Crucis" from the *Speculum Ecclesiae*.[26] Psalm iv is, according to the Sarum Breviary, to be read daily at the office of Compline, and verse 7 is expanded as an antiphon for St. Stephen's Day.[27] Langland himself quotes the fourth psalm twice in Passus XV (ll. 79, 250).

For the suggestion to be valid, however, this biblical reference must not only be a "half-line in Latin" containing a reference to a lamp, with a transitive interpretation; it must also fit Langland's context. What, then, of "Kynde loue coueiteth nouȝte . no catel but speche"? The work of Knowlton, Fr. Dunning, and Erzgräber should make the student of *Piers Plowman* extremely wary of assigning to *kynde* the meaning of Modern English *natu-*

---

est, vel recuperata. ... Vel ita, ut *intransitive* [my italics] legatur, lumen vultus tui, id est luminosus vultus tuus, et illuminans nos, scilicet imago per quam cognoscetis nunc in aenigmate, in futuro prout es."
[24] Charlton T. Lewis and Charles Short, *A Latin Dictionary* (Oxford, 1958), p. 1084.
[25] *PL.* 177, 794.
[26] Honorius of Autun, *PL.* 172, 941.
[27] Vol. I, 13; ccii.

ral, thus making *kynde loue* refer to the natural affection binding together friends and kindred.[28] Instead, one might look elsewhere in *Piers* for a clue to its meaning in the passage under consideration. In Passus III, Conscience's rejection of Lady Meed includes a prophecy of a kingdom of truth and peace.

> Ac kynde loue shal come ʒit . and conscience togideres,
> And make of lawe a laborere . such loue shal arise,
> And such a pees amonge the peple . and a perfit trewthe,
> That Iewes shal wene in here witte . and waxen wonder glade,
> That Moises or Messie . be come in-to erthe,
> And haue wonder in here hertis . that men beth so trewe.
>
> (III, 297–302)

Interestingly enough, this passage is concluded with a prophetic riddle involving the middle of the moon. However, the point at hand is the connotations of the expression "kynde loue". The love described here is a good deal more than the natural affection of friends and kinsmen. It is *kynde* or *natural* because all obstructions and obstacles to its proper course have been removed. Such unobstructed love or charity *coueiteth*, desires, *no catel,* no possessions; that is, such love is devoid of self-interest. According to Passus XIII, however, such love does desire one thing – *speche,* expression of itself. Love, whether carnal or spiritual, seeks to express itself, to become manifest; it cannot exist without an object, and it seeks to communicate itself to this object. At this level of meaning, "With half a laumpe lyne in latyn . *ex vi transicionis*" may be taken as a prepositional phrase used adjectivally, modifying *kynde loue.* That is: Unobstructed charity, stamped not only with reason but also with grace, desires nothing but self-expression.

Besides this primary meaning, these two lines have some fairly obvious overtones. Since Knowlton and Erzgräber have established the point that Langland often uses *kynde* as a synonym for God the Creator, one could regard *kynde loue* as that love characteris-

---

[28] E. C. Knowlton, "Nature in Middle English", *JEGP*, XX (1921), pp. 186-207. T. P. Dunning, *Piers Plowman: An Interpretation of the A-text* (New York, 1937), pp. 42-67. Willi Erzgraber, *William Langlands Piers Plowman* (Heidelberg, 1957), pp. 43-47.

tic of the Creator. This love desires nothing but to express itself in *speche*, the Word made flesh of John i, 14. Such a comparison between the Incarnation and the articulation of a word was a commonplace by the fourteenth century. It is found, for example, in the eleventh chapter of the fifteenth book of St. Augustine on the Trinity; and it underlies much of Book IX of the same treatise.[29] St. Bonaventura uses the same comparison with some frequency.[30] If this traditional comparison underlies the passage from Langland, then "With half a laumpe lyne in latyn , *ex vi transicionis*" might express a concomitant result of the Incarnation. The two lines would be paraphrased: "The love of God the Father desired nothing but to become the Word; with this act the Creation was stamped not only with reason, but also with grace." Or, perhaps better, the half lamp line might modify *covets* by differentiating the two great "speeches" of God: "God the Father desired to become manifest (i.e., to become *speche*) by (*with*) not only the *fiats* of the creation, which He stamped with reason; but also by (*with*) the Word of the new creation, which He stamped with grace."

If this somewhat labored interpretation of the two lines is correct, they are too concentrated to lend themselves to a short, inclusive paraphrase. *Kynde loue* is both unobstructed charity and the love of the Father, both of which are devoid of self-interest, desiring only expression. The first half of Ps. iv, 7, read transitively, is a synedoche for the great acts of the creation and the redemption of the world. Three possibilities for the relationship between the two lines have been offered above: that the half lamp line modifies or characterizes *kynde loue*; that it describes the result of the Incarnation; and that it differentiates the two great "speeches" of God – the Creation and Redemption. There is still a fourth possible reading.

Ps. iv, 7 was conventionally connected with the denarius stamped with Caesar's image [31] mentioned in Matt. xxii, 17-21, which concludes: "Reddite ergo quae sunt Caesaris, Caesari; et quae

---

[29]   *PL*. 42, 1071-1073; 967-972.
[30]   Vol. I, pp. 481, 558; Vol. IX, pp. 107, 110.
[31]   For examples, see commentaries cited in notes 22 and 23, above.

sunt Dei, Deo." Having made such a connection, St. Augustine
says of Ps. iv, 7: "Quemadmodum Caesar a uobis *exigit* [my
italics] impressionem imaginis suae, sic et Deus; ut quemadmodum
illi redditur nummus, sic Deo anima lumine uultus euis illustrata
atque signata." [32] A fourth possible interpretation of Langland's
lines, then, would be that the love of the Father desires only two
things of mankind: *speche*, or man's acknowledgement, in prayer
and praise, of God's sovereign power and love; and a soul rendered to Him re-created in the image of Christ, just as Caesar exacts
the denarius stamped with his image. Rather than espouse any
one of these four possibilities as the correct one, it is preferable,
I think, to submit them all, any one or all of which Langland may
have had in mind.

Some attention must now be given to the remainder of the passage. The next four lines read:

> I bere ther in a bouste . Dowel ybound
> In a signe of the Saterday . that sette firste the kalendare,
> And al the witte of the Wednesday . of the nexte wyke after;
> The myddel of the mone . is the miȝte of bothe.
>
> (XIII, 152–155)

(Goodridge's decision to regard them as a continuation of Patience's speech was adopted.[33]) Patience says that in a *bouste* or
box she carries Dowel bound up with the sign of the Saturday
that first set the calendar and with the wisdom of the Wednesday
of the next week, the power of both springing from the full moon.
To solve Patience's riddle, it is necessary, first of all, to translate
Saturday into seventh day, and Wednesday into fourth day. The
seventh day which first set the calendar would be the seventh day
of creation which set the calendar of human time by marking the
close of the divine creative acts. It also set or determined the
calendar by fixing the length of a week – the point where the
reckoning of days recommenced. In certain tracts on charity
the seven days of creation are often correlated with the seven

---

[32] *Enarrationes in Psalmos: Corpus Christianorum Series Latina,* Vol.
XXXVIII, p. 17.
[33] P. 306.

cardinal and theological virtues, the seventh day with charity.[34]
Relying on this tradition, one can regard the Saturday which
first set the calendar as a figure of charity. Line 153 might be
paraphrased: "In a signification of the seventh day of creation
– charity." By saying the *wit* or wisdom of Wednesday, Langland makes his second day an explicit figure of wisdom. Here
again he may be drawing on the tracts on charity in which the
fourth day is connected with prudence or worldly wisdom.[35] However, a problem arises since he is clearly not speaking of the fourth
day of creation, but rather of the fourth day of the *nexte wyke
after*. The solution lies, I think, in the *transitive* gloss of Ps. iv, 7,
the half lamp line, where emphasis is laid on the creation and on
the re-creation.

Inevitably, comparisons were drawn by the medieval exegetes
between the events of the creation and the events of the re-creation. For example, just as Adam was created on the sixth day, so
Christ was conceived on the sixth day.[36] Just as God rested on the
seventh day, so Christ rested in the tomb on the seventh day.[37]
The creation of the moon on the fourth day was frequently connected with the Passion or with Easter.[38] St. Bonaventura compares
at some length the seven words of the creation with the seven
"words" of the re-creation.[39] A list, given by Peter of Blois, of
the seven *days* of the re-creation is particularly significant. They
are the Conception, the Nativity, the Preaching, the Passion, the
Resurrection, the Ascension, and the Glorification.[40] According
to this scheme, the fourth *day* of re-creation would be the Passion.

[34] *Tractatus De Charitate, PL.* 184, 608-609. Aelred of Rievaulx, *Speculum Charitatis, PL.* 195, 536. Peter of Blois, *De Charitate Dei et Proximi,
PL.* 207, 906-908.
[35] For example: "Prudentia quasi dies quartus faciat, quasi scientiae
lumen erumpat, et inter facienda et non facienda discernens, dividat inter
diem et noctem, quatenus lumen sapientiae velut solis splendor effulgeat:
lux vero scientiae spiritualis, quae in quibusdam deficit, quasi lux lunae
minor appareat" (*Tractatus De Charitate: PL.* 184, 613).
[36] Honorius of Autun, *Hexameron (PL.* 172, 266).
[37] Rabanus Maurus, *Commentaria in Genesim, PL.* 107, 465.
[38] Honorius of Autun, *PL.* 172, 257. Alanus De Insulis, *Distinctiones:
PL.* 210, 842.
[39] Vol. IX, pp. 182-183.
[40] *PL.* 207, 913. See also *PL.* 184, 613.

The connection between wisdom and the Passion lies in the medieval concept that at the Passion God *outwitted* Satan; that is, that Satan unwittingly committed an injustice in occasioning the suffering and death of Jesus because he was not fully aware of who Jesus was; and by inveigling Satan into committing an injustice, God broke Satan's power.[41] Thus, the "Wednesday of the nexte wyke after" is the Passion seen as the fourth day of the second great week in Christian history, the *week* of the re-creation.

Since Easter must occur on the first Sunday after the first full moon following the vernal equinox, and since the moon is full half way through its cycle, "the myddel of the mone" becomes a fairly patent reference to Easter.[42] That the *might* of both the sign of the Saturday and wisdom of the next Wednesday springs from the full moon, seems to mean that neither the creation, completed on the seventh day, nor the Passion, represented by the fourth day of the next *week*, has any ultimate meaning from the human point of view without the Resurrection. In addition, the sign of the Saturday (God's love) and the wit of the Wednesday (God's wisdom), both incarnate in Christ, were manifested and confirmed in the Resurrection.[43] The riddle also has a moral application for the individual Christian. He who would do well must seek to know God (wisdom) and to love Him (charity). These two great Christian goals can only be accomplished through the power of the risen Christ.

In this passage, then, Patience says that Dowel is bound up with wisdom and love. This would seem to represent a conflation of two accounts of Dowel, Dobet, and Dobest given a few lines earlier in the poem. In Passus XIII, lines 127-128, Clergy quotes Piers as saying that Dowel and Dobet are two infinities which together discover Dobest. In lines 137-138 Patience himself says that to learn is Dowel, to teach is Dobet, and to love one's enemies is Dobest. Surely the infinities learning (Dowel) and teaching (Dobet) are components of wisdom; and wisdom, knowledge

[41] Langland makes frequent allusions to this idea in Passus XVIII. See R. E. Kaske, "Gigas the Giant in *Piers Plowman*", *JEGP*, LVI (1957), pp. 182-183.
[42] Goodridge, p. 307.
[43] For the biblical statement of a similar concept, see I Cor. xv, 14, 17.

of God, does "discover" love of God. As St. Augustine puts it, love is a consequence of wisdom. That is, when something is known, it produces charity or cupidity by pleasing either spiritually or carnally.[44] Or, in terms of Patience's speech, the two infinities learning and teaching, which comprise wisdom, result in the ability to love one's enemies, the perfection of charity. Thus, Dowel, learning, is inseparably *ybound* with the other component of wisdom, teaching (Dobet), and both in turn are bound up with the perfection of charity, *Dilige inimicos* (Dobest).

Patience's speech may extend through line 171;[45] however, these lines do not exhibit a meaningful concentration of charity images, and thus have not been dealt with here. The lines which have been discussed are as cryptic as any in *Piers Plowman*. However, in the light of their traditional associations, they become not only intelligible, but profoundly meaningful.

It is fitting that Will's instruction in charity, begun by Lady Holy Church, should be continued by Patience. Will is characterized at the beginning of Passus XIII as nearly witless because of the trials and perplexities recorded in the earlier Passus. It is a medieval commonplace that charity manifests itself first of all as patience in adversity; this lesson in patience is one that Will must learn before he can contemplate charity in the vision of the tree.[46]

[44] See, for example, *De Trinitate*, Bk. IX, chap. viii (*PL*. 42, 967-968).
[45] Goodridge, p. 306.
[46] The portion of this chapter which deals with Patience's riddle has been previously published in *MLN*, LXXVI (1961), pp. 675-682. The author is grateful to the editor of *MLN* for permission to reprint this material here.

III

THE TREE OF CHARITY

Having concluded her enigmatic discussion, Patience, along with Conscience, goes forth as a pilgrim; together they bring about the regeneration of Haukyn, the active man. In the immediately following vision, Will encounters Anima, who tenders a lengthy discourse on charity. This discourse (XV, 145-339), depending in large measure on I Cor. xiii, is primarily a discussion of the manifestations of the spirit of charity in charitable acts. The use of figurative language – for the most part, of personification – is considerable; however, these figures are explicit enough, or their scriptural associations immediate enough, that there is little to be gained from a detailed analysis of their traditional nature. Moreover, my investigation of the traditional context of Anima's discourse has revealed little of consequence, nor has a significant pattern of traditional associations emerged as in the case of Lady Holy Church's speech.

However, when the dreamer himself expresses some dissatisfaction with Anima's discussion of charity (Ac ȝet I am in a were . what charite is to mene [XVI, 3]), Anima responds by introducing one of the most arresting configurations of charity to be found in *Piers*:

> "It is a ful trye tree", quod he . "trewly to telle.
> Mercy is the more ther-of . the myddel stokke is Reuthe.
> The leues ben Lele-Wordes . the lawe of Holycherche,
> The blosmes beth Boxome-Speche . and Benygne-Lokynge;
> Pacience hatte the pure tre . and pore symple of herte,
> And so, thorw god and thorw good men . groweth the frute
>   Charite."

"I wolde trauaille", quod I, "this tree to se . twenty hun-
    dreth myle,
And forto haue my fylle of that frute . forsake al other
    saulee.
Lorde", quod I, "if any wiʒte wyte . whider-oute it groweth?"
"It groweth in a gardyne", quod he . "that god made hym-seluen,
Amyddes mannes body . the more is of that stokke;
Herte hatte the herber . that it in groweth,
And *Liberum-Arbitrium* . hath the londe to ferme,
Vnder Piers the Plowman . to pyken it and to weden it."
"Piers the Plowman!" quod I tho . and al for pure ioye
That I herde nempne his name . anone I swouned after,
And laye longe in a lone dreme . and atte laste me thouʒte,
That Pieres the Plowman . al the place me shewed,
And bad me toten on the tree . on toppe and on rote.
With thre pyles was it vnder-piʒte . I perceyued it sone.
"Pieres", quod I, "I preye the . whi stonde thise piles here?"
                                        (XVI, 4–24)

Piers explains that the three staves, representing primary attributes of the three persons of the Trinity, protect the tree against
the "winds" of the world, the flesh, and the devil (ll. 25-52).
Will continues to question Piers about the three staves and where
they grew originally; Piers' answer is abrupt, and his manner dis-
courages further questions about the staves (ll. 53-65). Will returns his attention to the tree of charity and asks Piers to describe
its fruit (ll. 65-66). Piers' answer and the conclusion of the vision
of the tree follow:

"Here now bineth", quod he tho . "if I nede hadde,
Matrymonye I may nyme . a moiste fruit with-alle.
Thanne contenence is nerre the croppe . as calewey bastarde,
Thanne bereth the croppe kynde fruite . and clenneste of alle,
Maydenhode, angeles peres . and rathest wole be ripe,
And swete with-oute swellyng . soure worth it neuere."
I prayed Pieres to pulle adown . an apple, and he wolde,
And suffre me to assaye . what sauoure it hadde.
And Pieres caste to the croppe . and thanne comsed it to crye,
And wagged Wydwehode . and it wepte after.
And whan it neued Matrimoigne . it made a foule noyse,
That I had reuth whan Piers rogged . it gradde so reufulliche.
For euere as thei dropped adown . the deuel was redy,
And gadred hem alle togideres . bothe grete and smale,

Adam and Abraham . and Ysay the prophete,
Sampson and Samuel . and seynt Iohan the baptiste;
Bar hem forth boldely . no body hym letted,
And made of holy men his horde . in lymbo inferni,
There is derkenesse and drede . and the deuel maister.
And Pieres for pure tene . that o pile he lauȝte,
And hitte after hym . happe how it myȝte,
Filius, bi the Faber wille . and frenesse of *Spiritus Sancti,*
To go robbe that raggeman . and reue the fruit fro hym.
(XVI, 67–89)

The traditional Christian background of this passage has already received a good bit of scholarly attention. For example, in treating of the tree Dorothy L. Owen makes limited use of St. Bonaventura.[1] Mabel Day calls attention to a tree in Duns Scotus which she believes Langland to be imitating.[2] E. Talbot Donaldson uses certain writings of St. Bernard of Clairvaux in his explication of the equivalent passage in the C-text.[3] Robertson and Huppé cite the works of pseudo-Hugh of St. Victor, Bede, Gregory, St. Bonaventura, Martin of Tours, and Bruno Astensis in their account to the tree.[4] Finally, Morton W. Bloomfield attempts to demonstrate the influence of Joachim of Fiore in Langland's description of the tree of charity.[5]

Before re-examining the immediate background of Langland's configuration, however, one should call attention to a general tendency among medieval exegetes and ecclesiastics to employ the figure of the tree in a variety of allegorical significations. For example, Hugh of St. Cher identifies penitence with a tree whose root is contrition, whose branches are good works, whose foliage is confession, and whose fruit is satisfaction.[6] Rabanus Maurus lists a number of trees representing various virtues which should flourish within the individual Christian.[7] Vincent of Beauvais de-

---

[1] *PPL: A Comparison with Some Earlier and Contemporary French Allegories* (London, 1912), p. 124.
[2] "Duns Scotus and 'Piers Plowman'", *RES,* III (1927), pp. 333-334.
[3] Pp. 188-191.
[4] Pp. 191-196.
[5] "*PPL* and the Three Grades of Chastity", *Anglia,* LXXVI (1958), pp. 227-253.
[6] Vol. VI, fol. 10ʳ.
[7] *PL.* 108, 553.

scribes at length the flower and fruit of one of these trees, the tree of wisdom.[8] In the *Allegoriae* of pseudo-Rabanus, *lignum* is given six significations: *Christus, Crux, Incarnata Sapientia, Humilis, Cor hominis, Deliciae spirituales*.[9] Moreover, such allegorical trees are frequently connected with charity. For example, Hugh of St. Cher comments on the spiritual tree of the inner man rooted in charity, and bearing the fruit of good works and the foliage of good words.[10] Langland's configuration of the tree of charity, then, seems to stem first of all from this general consciousness of the tree as a vehicle for Christian allegory.

Another medieval tendency should also be mentioned. Eleanor Simmons Greenhill has done a notable study of the symbol of the tree in the Christian tradition.[11] Here, and in other studies of the symbol of the tree, the tendency of the medieval mind to fuse the various Christian meanings of the tree is apparent.[12] The controlling idea of the ensuing discussion is that Langland's configuration is essentially eclectic, reflecting various trees of the Christian tradition – including the tree of Jesse, the tree of life or the tree of the cross, the tree of virtues, and the tree of the descent of mankind from Adam.

The whole configuration is extremely complex; and, like all successfully compressed poetic figures, it leads the reader's imagination in a number of different directions, which for the medieval reader would be largely controlled by the traditional associations of the figure. Because of this complexity, it seems advisable to approach the configuration of the B-text through its more explicit counterpart in the C-text. Passus XIX of the C-text includes the lines,

Euene in the myddes . an ympe, as hit were,
That hihte *Ymago-dei* . graciousliche hit growede.

8 *Speculum Historiale*, Bk. XXVI, chap. 81.
9 *PL*. 112, 985-986.
10 Vol. VII, fol. 173ʳ.
11 "The Child in the Tree: A Study of the Cosmological Tree in Christian Tradition", *Traditio*, X (1954), pp. 323-371.
12 See, for example, D. W. Robertson, Jr., "The Doctrine of Charity in Medieval Literary Gardens: A Topical Approach through Symbolism and Allegory", *Speculum*, XXVI (1951), pp. 24-27. Greenhill, pp. 349-369.

Thenne gan ich asken what hit hyhte . and he me sone tolde –
"The tree hihte Trewe-loue", quath he . "the trinite hit
  sette."   (II.6-9)

Skeat equates *ympe* and *tree* in his comment on this passage, suggesting that *Ymago-dei* and *Trewe-loue* are different names for
the tree.[13] He admits, however, that the ME meaning of *ympe* is
"graft", "shout", or "scion"; and the *OED* similarly defines
the term as meaning basically that which has grown out of something else or which is grafted onto something else, with special
reference to plants or trees. Moreover, the term is used elsewhere
in *Piers* in the clear sense of "graft" (B, V, 136-138). There
seems to be ample justification, then, for regarding *Ymago-dei*
as a graft or shoot of the tree of *Trewe-loue*, rather than identifying the two as Skeat does. If such a distinction is valid, the traditional associations of the passage may be clarified by referring
to an interpretation of Cant. ii, 3, "Sicut malus inter ligna silvarum, sic Dilectus meus inter filios", exemplified by the comment of Hugh of St. Cher:

Silvarum enim ligna unius tantum naturae sunt, quia tota de terra
oriuntur, sine alterius arboris insitione. Malus vero quasi duplicis
naturae est. Nam truncum habet a terra productum, surculum aliunde
accipit venientem, quae conjuncta per insitionem, unam arborem
faciunt tantum. Sic omnes homines praeter Christum unius naturae
tantum sunt, scilicet, humanae; Christus vero duplicis, humanae
scilicet et divinae. Humanitati enim quasi trunco, Divinitas quasi
surculus desuper veniens in unitate personae inserta est et unita.[14]

Thus Hugh interprets the apple tree as a prefiguration of the double nature of Christ, while the *surculus* or graft is specifically
identified with the divinity of Christ. Moreover, the name of the
graft, according to Langland, is *Ymago-dei;* and while this term
can have a variety of applications, the Apostle himself identifies
it with Christ (II Cor. iv, 4). The full implication of the figure
of the grafted tree, then, is probably that the tree of true love can
only flourish when it is "grafted" with God's image, consum-
mately personified in Christ. This indication that standard com-

---

[13] Vol. II, p. 235, n. 6.
[14] Vol. III, fol. 114v.

mentaries on the *malus* of Canticles underlie Langland's configuration is supported to some extent by other less exact parallels.
For example, the shade of the apple tree protects the Christian
from the triple heat of God's anger, of riotous excess, and of mal-
ice,[15] and the three piles secure the tree of charity against the
winds of the world, the flesh, and the devil.

Just as Hugh equates the apple tree of Canticles with the *virga
de radice Jesse* in the same passage,[16] so in a larger context the
image of the grafted tree is connected with a figure exceedingly
well known in the Middle Ages, that of the tree of Jesse. This
figure originates in Isa. xi, 1-3: "Et egredietur virga de radice
Jesse, et flos de radice ejus ascendet. Et requiescet super eum spiritus Domini: spiritus sapientiae et intellectus, spiritus consilii et
fortitudinis, spiritus scientiae et pietatis, et replebit eum spiritus
timoris Domini." As conventionally represented in medieval art,
this figure shows a tree rising from or near Jesse – usually recumbent – with some representation of the Virgin or Christ at
its summit, and with a dove or an aureole of seven doves representing the gifts of the Holy Spirit.[17] The connection between the
malus of Canticles and the tree of Jesse will be clarified by reference to Lydgate's translation of Guillaume de Guilleville's *Le
pèlerinage de l'âme*, a work written before Langland's day and
translated afterwards. Here the tree of Jesse is described as a
grafted apple tree (our blessed lady grafted upon the stock of St.
Anne) – a tree, moreover, illuminating all who see it with sovereign charity.[18] Further paralleling the passage cited above from
the C-text, the translator uses various forms of *ymp* in connection
with the tree of Jesse. In addition, this work lays emphasis on
the fact that the tree of Adam's progeny bears good fruit only as
the result of having been grafted with a shoot from the tree of

---

[15] Vol. III, fol. 114v.

[16] *Ibid.*

[17] Arthur Watson, *The Early Iconography of the Tree of Jesse* (London,
1934), p. 1. Watson does not mention the doves at this point, but in fully
developed representations of this figure, they were the rule rather than the
exception.

[18] *The Book of the Pylgremage of the Sowle* (London, 1483), fols. 53v-
59r.

Jesse; such an emphasis parallels Langland's basic idea that the tree of true love flourishes only when it is grafted with God's image.

The tree of Jesse is used predominantly in the Middle Ages as a prefiguration of the Virgin Mary, just as in de Guilleville; an important secondary significance is as a type of Christ.[19] In its primary use as a type of the Virgin, the tree of Jesse resembles Langland's tree in that its crowning fruit is virginity. In its secondary use as a type of Christ, it may underlie the detail from the C-text that the tree of true love is grafted with Christ, the *Ymagodei*.[20] In addition, Langland's tree of charity arises from the midst of man's body (XVI, 14), and the tree of Jesse is generally depicted as arising from the body of Jesse, recumbent.

The tree of Jesse may have influenced Langland's tree in still another way. Structurally, the vision of the tree of charity occupies a key position in the narrative of Will's pilgrimage. As a result of this vision the dreamer's quest for Dowel, Dobet, and Dobest shifts to a quest for Piers the ploughman. And this new quest leads directly to Will's encounters with Faith, Hope and Charity – encounters which culminate in the climactic account in Passus XVIII of the Passion and Harrowing of Hell. Thus the primary importance of the vision of the tree as a major turning point, perhaps the major turning point, in the action of the poem cannot be denied. As a manuscript illumination, the tree of Jesse was conventionally used to occupy similarly significant positions.[21] Because of the unique nature of this figure – rising as it does from the Old Testament Jesse to the Virgin and Christ – it was used to join matter traditionally connected with the old dispensation to matter traditionally connected with the new. Dodwell notes the use of the tree of Jesse to knit together the so-called Old and

[19] Watson, p. 80.
[20] However, *Imago-dei* is sometimes identified with virginity. See, for example, Hugh of St. Cher, Vol. VII, fol. 91ʳ.
[21] F. Harrison, *Treasures of Illumination: English MSS of the Fourteenth Century* (London, 1937), plates ix, xiii; Donald Drew Egbert, *The Tickshill Psalter and Related MSS* (New York, 1940), p. 21, and plate iv. In these instances the tree of Jesse is the central illumination of the *Beatus* page of the psalter.

New Testament sequences in several psalters; [22] and Watson cites examples in which the tree of Jesse is used as an initial illumination of the first chapter of Matthew.[23] If such a function of the tree of Jesse underlies Langland's vision of the tree of charity, then it is significant that the vision concludes with a *vita Christi*. Moreover, though it would be untenable to press the parallel too closely, in the passus preceding the vision the dreamer is perplexed with universal questions answered only by riddles and partial truths in a manner which might suggest the state of man under the old dispensation. Thus the medieval consciousness of the tree of Jesse may contribute to Langland's tree of charity in a number of ways, not the least of which is the structural position in the poem of the tree of charity.

Another characteristic of the fully developed figure of the tree of Jesse is that, like Langland's figure, it is expanded, conflated, eclectic, even encyclopedic. For example, in the fourteenth-century *Vaux Psalter*, the illumination of the *Beatus* page shows the sleeping Jesse surmounted by a conventional depiction of the crucifixion including the Virgin and St. John, surmounted by a depiction of the Virgin and Child, surmounted by a depiction of Christ enthroned as God.[24] A ceiling painting at St. Michael's, Hildesheim, shows a fully developed Tree of Jesse in its central panel, including Jesse, David, Solomon, the Virgin, Christ, and the Old Testament kings and prophets. Immediately beneath the central panel is a depiction of the temptation in the Garden of Eden, and the side panels and medallions show the four evangelists and their symbolic beasts, the archangels, the rivers of paradise, and the cardinal virtues.[25] However, as in the case of the illumination from the *Vaux Psalter* cited above, the Tree of Jesse was most frequently connected with the *lignum vitae* of Gen. ii, 9. This tree planted by God in the midst of the Garden of Eden was conventionally regarded as the most significant Old Testament type of the cross and of Christ's sacrifice. A few citations

[22] C. R. Dodwell, *The Canterbury School of Illumination, 1066-1200* (Cambridge, 1954), pp. 99-100.
[23] Pp. 110, 112, plate xxiii.
[24] Harrison, plate xiii.
[25] Watson, pp. 125-127, plate xxvii.

will demonstrate the traditional association between the tree of Jesse and the *lignum vitae/crucis*. For example, Peter Damian's sermon, *De exaltatione Sanctae Crucis*, begins: "De virga Iesse devenimus ad virgam crucis et principium redemptionis fine concludimus." [26] The opening text of the sermon on the same subject in the *Speculum Ecclesiae* is: "Radix Jesse stabit in signum populorum" (Isa. xi, 10).[27] In the *Vaux Psalter* the fruit of the tree of Jesse is Christ crucified.[28] The tree of Jesse and the *lignum vitae* are conflated and associated with charity in the thirteenth-century *Sommes des vices et des vertues* of Brother Laurent.[29] The echoes of the tree of Jesse already proposed for Langland's tree, then, suggest the possibility of a further association between Langland's tree and the *lignum vitae*; and this possibility seems greatly increased by the prominent place of the *lignum vitae* in the Christian tradition as a type of the cross, along with the medieval tendency to conflate all the trees within the tradition.

Eph. iii, 16-19, which the commentators conventionally connect with the tree of life or the cross, reads:

Ut det vobis secundum divitias gloriae suae, virtute corroborari per Spiritum ejus in interiorem hominem, Christum habitare per fidem in cordibus vestris: in charitate radicati, et fundati, ut possitis comprehendere cum omnibus sanctis, quae sit latitudo, et longitudo, et sublimitas, et profundum: scire etiam supereminentem scientiae charitatem, ut impleamini in omnem plenitudinem Dei.

Peter Lombard, in commenting on this passage, makes the usual connection with the cross: "Et sciendum quia in his verbis figura et mysterium crucis ostenditur." At the same time, he makes explicit the figure connecting the tree with charity: "Oro etiam ut *in charitate radicati*, id est firmiter plantati, ad similitudinem

---

[26]   *PL.* 144, 761, cited by Watson, p. 53.
[27]   *PL.* 172, 1001.
[28]   See n. 24 above.
[29]   Ann Brooks Tysor, ed., "Sommes des vices et des vertues". Unpublished M.A. thesis (Chapel Hill, 1949), pp. 88-89: "La racine de cest arbre [tree of life] c'est la tres grant amour et l'outrageuse amour charite Dieus le pere. Donc il nous am tant que pour son malves serf rachater il donna son douz filz et le livra a mort et a torment. De cest racine parle le prophete et dit que une verge iscroit de la racine Ysse. Cest mot Ysse valt autant comme baisier d'amour."

arboris." He then equates *latitudo* with the transverse member of
the cross, which, he says, pertains to good works; *longitudo* with
the upright member of the cross between the ground and the
transverse member, which signifies *perseverantiam; altitudo* with
the upright member above the transverse member, which signifies the expectation of better things; and *profundum* with that
portion of the upright member hidden in the earth, which signifies grace freely given. The whole argument *is* reiterated and
summarized:

Quae sit latitudo in operibus charitatis, quae extenditur usque ad
inimicos diligendos, sicut Christus fecit, qui oravit pro inimicis quod
ostensum in cruce sua fuit, quae in altum tensa est a dextra in sinis-
tram, ubi manus fixae per quas opera signantur, quae in hilaritate
decet esse, et quae longitudo charitatis, scilicet quod usque in finem
durare debet. Unde dicitur de Christo: *Cum dilexisset suos, usque in
finem dilexit illos.* Quod significatum est per longitudinem crucis, a
sursam usque deorsum. Et quae sublimitas, charitatis, id est quo
tendat charitas, scilicet ad aeternam beatitudinem, quae notatur per
partem crucis superpositam, et quod profundum, charitatis quod
totum portat, ut pars crucis fixa in terra, scilicet in abscondito quod
non videtur, id est misericordia Dei, quae occulto Dei judicio pro-
venit, per quam charitas in nobis longa, lata est, scilicet et alta.[30]

This standard interpretation of the passage from Ephesians has
rather far-reaching implications for Langland's description of the
tree of charity. As noted above, the relationship between charity
and the image of a tree, implicit in the scriptural passage, becomes
explicit in the commentary. In the second place, the commentator
connects *longitudo*, the visible portion of the upright member of
the cross below the transverse member, with *perseverantia*. A
relationship or approximate equation exists between *perseverantia*
and ME *pacience*; and Langland says, "Pacience hatte the pure
tre" (XVI, 8). "Pure tre" is rendered by standard translators of
Piers as "tree itself",[31] and the expression certainly could embody

---

[30] *Collectanea in Epist. D. Pauli ad Ephes., PL.* 192, 192-194. For essentially the same commentary, see, for example, Bruno the Carthusian,
PL. 153, 332-333, and Rabanus Maurus, *PL.* 112, 424.
[31] Goodridge, p. 236; Nevill Coghill, *Visions from Piers Plowman* (London, 1953), p. 85, l. 7.

the idea of the essential tree unadorned by branches, foliage, flowers, or fruit: in short, the trunk or main stem. If this interpretation is correct, then Langland's detail that the "pure tre" of the tree of charity is "pacience" depends upon a conventional connection between the main longitudinal section of the tree of the cross and *perseverantiam*. Even more convincing is the fact that Gilbert of Hoyt connects the longitudinal section of the cross with *perseverantiam* or *patientiam*: "Cedrus arbor longitudine praestans alius arboribus, longitudinem crucis, id est, perseverantiam significat, sive patientiam." [32] Moreover, Peter glosses *profundum charitatis* as that portion of the cross buried in the earth, which signifies God's mercy whereby charity is long, broad, and high in the Christian. Langland's tree of charity, like the *lignum vitae* as interpreted by Peter Lombard, is rooted in mercy and grows *in nobis* into the breadth, length, and height of charity. Considerable negative evidence supports the suggestion that Langland's figure of the root of mercy may have this rather specific traditional association; most of the trees of the Christian tradition used *in bono* are rooted either in charity or humility.[33] Langland's connection of the "middle stock" of the tree of charity with pity could be an extension of this figure of the root of mercy.

Will's desire to taste the fruit of the tree of charity (XVI, 10-11) may reflect another aspect of the tree of life, whose fruit confers salvation. According to Gilbert of Hoyt, for example, Christ, as the fruit of the cross, is to be understood as *salvatio*.[34] According to Hugh of St. Victor, Christ is the *lignum vitae,* and whoever feeds upon it will have eternal life.[35]

A more or less tropological interpretation of the *lignum vitae* should be mentioned in connection with Langland's figure. This is the tree of wisdom, the tree of life which flourishes in the hearts of the saints. Of this tree Hugh of St. Victor says:

[32] *In Cantica Sermo XXIX, PL.* 184, 151.
[33] For examples: Adolf Katzenellenbogen, *Allegories of the Virtues and Vices in Medieval Art,* trans. Alan J. P. Crick (London, 1939), plates xxxviii and xli; St. Bernard of Clairvaux, *Sermones in Cantica, PL.* 183, 935; Hugh of St. Cher, Vol. I, fol. 2r.
[34] *Vitis Mystica, PL.* 184, 733.
[35] *Allegoriae in Vetus Testamentum, PL.* 175, 639.

Hoc est igitur vere lignum vitae verbum Patris in excelsis sapientia Dei, quae in cordibus sanctorum tanquam in paradiso invisibili per timorem seminatur, per gratiam rigatur, per dolorem moritur, per fidem radicatur, per devotionem germinat, per compunctionem oritur, per desiderium crescit, per charitatem roboratur, per spem viret; per circumspectionem frondet, et expandit ramos, per disciplinam floret, per virtutem fructificat, per patientiam maturescit, per mortem carpitur, per contemplationem cibat.[36]

This tree, strengthened with charity, like Langland's tree grows in the heart. Moreover, planted in this unseen paradise through the wisdom of God, it would seem to represent the union between God and His saints, which would be the goal of Will's quest and, indeed, of all spiritual quests. Altogether, then, it seems clear that the *lignum vitae*, as developed in standard commentaries, contributes even more to Langland's tree of charity than does the tree of Jesse.

The first part of Will's vision of the tree of charity is predominated by the description of the three staves, an explicit figure of the Trinity and thus not germane to this study. However, by line 65 the attention of the dreamer has returned to the tree of charity itself, specifically to its fruit.

> "Here now bineth", quod he Piers tho . "if I nede hadde,
> Matrymonye I may nyme . a moiste fruit with-alle.
> Thanne contenence is nerre the croppe . as calewey bastarde,
> Thanne bereth the croppe kynde fruite . and clenneste of alle,
> Maydenhode, angeles peres . and rathest wole be ripe,
> And swete with-oute swellyng . soure worth it neuere."
>
> (XVI, 67–72)

This description of the fruit of the tree of charity depends upon standard commentaries on Matt. xiii, 3-8, the parable of the sower whose seed fell along the wayside, upon stony ground, among thorns, and finally upon good ground – the last of which alone brought forth fruit, some a hundredfold, some sixtyfold, and some thirtyfold. Of the fruitful seed the *Glossa Ordinaria* says, "*Et facit fructum*; tricesimum ostendit ordinem conjugatorum: sequentes mandatum Dei; fructus LX. ordine viduarum, perseverentiam

---

[36] *De Arca Noe Morali*, Bk. II, chap. xviii, *PL.* 176, 646. The figure of the tree of life underlies all of Book III of this same work.

in Domino; fructus centesimus, hoc sunt ordines martyrum, monachorum vel virginum." [37] The connection between charity and the threefold fruit of chastity can be clarified from standard commentators, for example, Denis the Carthusian:

Alia vero semina coelestis verbi, ceciderunt in *terram bonam,* id est cor fidele, docile atqui tractabile; *et dabant fructum,* id est, in opus bonum creverunt, sed diversimode secundum diversam dispositionem cordum recipientium ea: ideo subditur, *aliud* semen, id est quoddam verbum Dei, dedit fructum *centesimum,* id est, habuit opus perfectum: sicut in spiritualibus, divinis atqui heroicis viris. Talis est fructus castitates in virginibus. *Aliud* semen protulit fructum sexagesimum, id est, opus proficiens habuit: sicut in his qui conantur quotidie tendere de virtute in virtutem, et de statu proficientium ad statum perfectorum pertingere. *Aliud* semen attulit fructum *tricesimum,* id est, opus bonum habuit, sed imperfectum, inchoativum, ac animale, ut in incipientibus. Porro, quod dicitur de fructu centesimo, specialiter solet referri ad statum virginalem; et quod dicitur de fructu sexagesimo ad statum vidualem; quod vero de fructu tricesimo dicitur ad statum conjugalem.[38]

Various connections between this passage and Langland's configuration suggest themselves; for example, Anima says that the tree of charity grows in the *herber* of the heart (XVI, 15) while Denis equates *terram bonam* of Scripture with "cor fidele, docile atqui tractabile". Of greater significance, however, is the connection made by Denis between the threefold fruit and the perfection of good works. Denis' consideration of this point concludes: "quod multo perfectius fit in continentia virginale, quam viduali, et in viduali, quam conjugali. Unde dicit Apostolus: Virgo cogitat quae Domini sunt, ut sit sancta corpore et spiritu; quae autem nupta est, cogitat quae sunt mundi quomodo placeat vero; et divisa est".[39] Denis' allusion to the Apostle makes it clear that he regards the three grades of chastity as a kind of ladder stretching from earthly love to heavenly love. In other words, the three grades of chastity are synechdoches for the three forms charity may take: marriage, properly directed earthly love; widowhood, a mixture of earthly

[37] *PL.* 114, 880.
[38] Vol. XI, pp. 160a-161b.
[39] *Ibid.,* p. 162a.

and heavenly love; and virginity, pure heavenly love. St. Bonaventura explicitly connects charity with the three grades of chastity in a commentary on the three measures of leaven of Luke xiii,
21, a passage traditionally associated with the threefold fruit of
the parable of the sower.

Per *tria sata, triplex fructus*, ad quem caritas ordinat; unde Glossa:
Possunt in his *satis* illius dominici seminis fructus intelligi trigesimus
scilet, sexagesimus et centesimus, id est coniugatorum, continentium
et virginum; de quibus Matthaei decimo tertio: "Fructum affert, et
facit aliud quidem centesimum, alius sexagesimum, aluid vero trige-
simum." [40]

Thus, in the phraseology of St. Bonaventura, the three grades of
chastity are the "fruits", outward manifestations, of charity; and
many examples from medieval iconography could be cited in
which chastity is represented as the fruit of charity.[41] Therefore,
Langland is not multiplying contradictory details when in line 9
Anima states that the fruit of the tree is charity and in the passage under consideration Piers calls the fruit marriage, widowhood, and virginity. Piers' statement in the vision is, if anything,
more explicit than Anima's statement; and in any case there is
obviously so close a traditional relationship between charity and
the three grades of chastity that it is not surprising to find the two
used interchangeably. In addition, the comparative evaluation
obviously implied in Piers' description of the fruit reflects another
aspect of the Christian tradition touched on by Denis: the ladder
of the perfection of works.

The vision of the tree of charity concludes with an account of
the theft of the fruit by Satan:

I prayed Pieres to pulle adown . an apple, and he wolde,
And suffre me to assaye . what sauoure it hadde.
And Pieres caste to the croppe . and thanne comsed it to crye,
And wagged Wydwehode . and it wepte after.
And whan it meued Matrimoigne . it made a foule noyse,
That I had reuth whan Piers rogged . it gradde so reufulliche.
For euere as thei dropped adown . the deuel was redy,
And gadred hem alle togidere . bothe grete and smale,

----

40   Vol. VII, p. 349a.
41   For example, Katzenellenbogen, plate xxxviii, p. 66, n. 3, and plate xli.

Adam and Abraham . and Ysay the prophete,
Sampson and Samuel . and seynt Iohan the baptiste;
Bar hem forth holdely . no body hym letted,
And made of holy men his horde . in lymbo inferni,
There is derkenesse and drede . and the deuel maister.

(XVI, 73–85)

In characterizing the fruit of his tree as widely known characters
under the Old Law, Langland draws upon a number of traditions.
One of the more important of these is a development of the tree
of the cross typifying the salvation of the just of the Old Testament through Christ's sacrifice, according to which various figures of the Old Testament are depicted as the fruit of a cruciform
tree – as, for example, in a twelfth-century manuscript illumination from Regensburg.[42] Here the patriarchs, prophets, and mar-
tyrs are depicted in the convolutions of the branches below the
transverse member, while the apostles appear above it. Representations of the Virgin and of Christ appear as integral parts of the
cross itself. While this seems to be the predominant tradition underlying Langland's figure, Langland may also have been familiar
with other genealogical trees well known in the late Middle Ages.
For example, the fully developed figure of the tree of Jesse incor-
porates an extensive genealogy of Christ.[43] In addition, the Abbot
Joachim employs the figure of the tree to embody his conception
of the generations of the history of the world from Adam to the
consummation of the ages.[44] More germane to this study, however,
are conventional trees not only showing Adam's descent, but also
classifying his posterity according to the three grades of chastity.
Bloomfield reproduces one such illumination in his study of Langland's tree; it is found in a *Speculum Virginum* surviving at
Troyes.[45] A practically identical illumination appears in a *Specu-
culum Virginum* of uncertain date and provenance found in the
British Museum.[46] A tree with a threefold division rises above a

[42]   Albert Boeckler, *Die Regensburg-Prüfeninger Buchmalerei des XII.
und XIII. Jahrhunderts* (Munich, 1924), pl. xxxvii.
[43]   Watson, p. 142.
[44]   Marjorie Reeves, "The Arbores of Joachim of Fiore", *Papers of the
British School at Rome*, Vol. XXIV (1956), pp. 124-136.
[45]   Bloomfield, plate i.
[46]   B. M. Arundel 44, fol. 70ʳ.

pair of figures labelled Adam and Eve. The first division is labelled *fructus tricesimus conjugatorum* and in the convolutions of
its branches appear four pairs of figures: Abraham and Sara,
Zacharias and Elizabeth, Noah and his wife, and Job and his wife.
In the second division, labelled *fructus sexagesimus viduarum*,
appear four female figures identified as Debbora, Iudith, the wid-
ow who went to debtors' prison because of two pennies, and Anna.
In the third division, labelled *fructus centesimus virginum*, the
individual figures are not designated. Christ appears at the summit
of the tree, so that the figure is basically a tree of Adam's descent
until the time of Christ. This conflation of the tree of Adam's
descent with the three grades of chastity is analogous to the identification made by Langland between the three grades of chastity
and "Adam and Abraham . and Ysay the prophete, / Sampson
and Samuel . and seynt Iohan the baptiste" as fruit of the same
tree (XVI, 81-82). Langland uses the tradition of the tree of
Adam's descent as a transition to the *Vita Christi* which immediately follows in *Piers*: that is, the fact that Satan makes holy
men his "hord" in limbo explains the need for the Messiah.

Another tree of the Christian tradition should be mentioned
in connection with Langland's tree of charity. This is the tree of
virtues cited by Robertson and Huppé as explaining the tropological meaning of Langland's tree.[47] Basically, this tree is a graphic
representation of the way in which the cardinal and theological
virtues proceed from the antithesis of Superbia, Humilitas. While
Robertson and Huppé do not show detailed correspondences between the tree of virtues and Langland's tree, the primary fruit
of both trees is charity. And although Robertson and Huppé do
not discuss the legend surrounding the particular representation
of the tree of virtues which they reproduce, it explicitly connects
the tree of virtues with virginity. The legend reads in part:

> Quis sit amor pensat, qui dona perennia monstrat
> Vernant virginei fructu frente manipli.

Therefore, one is probably justified in regarding the tree of virtues as part of the background of Langland's tree of charity. It is

[47] Pp. 191-197.

doubtful, however, that this particular traditional tree should be given the prominence that Robertson and Huppé give it in their discussion of Langland's tree.[48]

Before concluding, one might make the miscellaneous point that, though it is not, strictly speaking, an image of charity, Langland's assigning Liberum Arbitrium custody of the tree of charity is in accordance with Christian tradition. According to St. Bonaventura, charity is dependent upon two things for its very existence: divine influence and a susceptible will; and when the will averts itself from God, charity is withdrawn.[49] The infusion of charity from God must be sustained by the human will. This conception accounts not only for free will's proprietorship, but also for Anima's statement that through God and good men grows the fruit charity (XVI, 9).

Langland's figure of the tree of charity has not been an easy one to deal with, because of both its own complexity and the complexity of the tradition of which it partakes – that of the metaphor of the tree in medieval Christianity. I have tried, however, to establish three points. First, I have tried to show that by its eclectic nature Langland's tree of charity reflects the Christian tradition, in which various trees were conflated with each other and with other traditional matter.[50] Secondly, I have tried to demonstrate that practically every detail of Langland's tree owes something to the Christian tradition: for example, the root of mercy and the "pure tre" of patience derive, I think, from the *lignum vitae/crucis*, while the arbor of man's heart probably derives

---

[48] Bloomfield takes special exception to Robertson and Huppé's emphasis on the tree of virtues. See *Speculum,* XXVII (1952), pp. 246-247.

[49] *Sententiarum, Opera,* Vol. III, p. 675: "Cum *esse* caritatis dependeat a duobus videlicet a Deo influente et a libero arbitrio suscipients; cum liberum arbitrium se a Deo avertit, caritas in semetipsa deficit. Et quia liberum arbitrium non se avertit nisi peccando, hinc est, quod caritas dicitur per peccatum expelli, non propter fortitudinem ipsius peccati agentis, sed propter defectionem ipsius liberi arbitrii suscipientis."

[50] The conflation of allegorical trees with other traditional matter has not been of primary concern in this study. As a case in point, however, other illuminations of B. M. Arundel 44 might be cited: folio 85r shows the tree of the cross as a ladder whereby man ascends to God; and folio 114v shows a tree of Jesse conflated with the seven pillars of the house of wisdom.

from a tropological interpretation of the *lignum vitae*. Finally, I
have tried to show that the medieval Christian tradition resolves
the apparent contradiction between the fruit of the tree as charity,
as the three grades of chastity, and as the just men of the old
dispensation: the three grades of chastity represent the fruits or
outward manifestations of charity, and the figures of the Old
Testament are sometimes classified according to the three grades
of chastity. In short, neither the individual details of the figure
of the tree of charity, nor the eclectic principle whereby they are
combined is original with Langland. Moreover, Langland is typi-
cally medieval when, in a key episode of his poem, he turns to the
figure of the tree, a central symbol in medieval Christianity. However, the exact combination of details is original, and results in
one of the most complex but meaningful images in medieval poetry. This is a supreme moment of vision in the poem; Will appre-
hends the tree of charity with all that it portends for the Christian,
but the moment passes, and he must continue his quest.

IV

THE GOOD SAMARITAN

The vision of the tree of charity concludes with a short *vita Christi* (XVI, 90-166). When Will awakens from this vision, he sets forth in search of Piers the ploughman (XVI, 167-171), encountering instead Abraham or Faith (XVI, 173), then *Spes* or Moses (XVII, 1), and then the Good Samaritan (XVII, 48). The use of the figure of the Good Samaritan lies well within the scope of this study, since Langland unmistakably uses him as a type of charity.[1] To appreciate fully Langland's use of the figure of the Good Samaritan, one must consider the poet's use of the parable as a whole; therefore, the attention of this chapter will be focused on lines 1 through 123 of Passus XVII: that is, from the point where Moses joins Abraham and Will to the point where the Good Samaritan begins to instruct Will in the doctrine of the Trinity.

Since the parable itself is brief, it is worth recalling in its entirety.

Homo quidam descendebat ab Ierusalem in Iericho, et incidit in latrones, qui etiam despoliaverunt eum: et plagis impositis abierunt semivivo relicto. Accidit autem ut sacerdos quidam descenderet eadem via: et viso illo praeterivit. Similiter et Levita, cum esset secus locum, et videret eum, pertransit. Samaritanus autem quidam iter faciens, venit secus eum: et videns eum, misericordia motus est. Et appropians alligavit vulnera eius, infundens oleum et vinum: et imponens illum in iumentum suum, duxit in stabulum et curam eius egit. Et altera die protulit duos denarios, et dedit stabulario, et ait: Curam illius

---

[1]   This identification is expressly stated nowhere in the poem. However, it is inevitable from the progression faith, hope, Good Samaritan.

habe: et quocumque supererogaveris, ego cum rediero reddam tibi. (Luxe x, 30–35)

The scriptural context of the parable should also be recalled. A lawyer has asked Christ a question similar to the one Will asked Lady Holychurch early in Passus I: "Master, what must I do to possess eternal life?" Christ queries the lawyer about the content of the law, whereupon the lawyer replies, "Thou shalt love the Lord thy God with thy whole heart, and with thy whole soul, and with all thy strength, and with all thy mind; and thy neigbor as thyself." [2] Christ's reply is, "This do, and thou shalt live." When the lawyer next asks for a definition of the term *neighbor*, Christ replies with the parable of the Good Samaritan. Thus, in its scriptural context, the parable is connected with charity; indeed, it is one of the Saviour's illustrations of the law of love. However, it is possible to show in a much more detailed way how Langland's use of this parable in connection with charity rests squarely on the traditional interpretation of the parable and related material.

The table that follows will demonstrate the conventional nature of the medieval interpretation of the parable and will indicate the dominant emphases of this interpretation.

	Glossa Ordinaria[3]	Rabanus Maurus[4]	Honorius of Autun[5]
Homo	Adam or Mankind	Adam or Mankind	Adam
Hierusalem		The city of heavenly peace	Joys of paradise
Hiericho		A place of change, toil and error	Defection of mankind
Latrones		The Devil and his ministers	Demons
Qui dispoliaverunt eum		Of his garment of innocence and immortality	Of the riches of paradise and of the garment of immortality
Plagae		Sins	Sin

[2]   It might be pointed out that in both Matthew and Mark it is Christ who delivers this summary of the law, accounting for its enormous authority in Christian thought.
[3]   *PL.* 114, 286-287.
[4]   *PL.* 110, 449-451.
[5]   *PL.* 172, 1059-1064.

76 THE GOOD SAMARITAN

Semivivus		Immortality was lost but not the rational sense	Spiritually dead
Sacerdos	He who proclaims law of God. Connected with Moses	Citizens of Jerusalem who failed to rescue their neighbor in the literal sense	The patriarchs who also travel the road of mortality
Levita	A type of the prophets		Prophets, also subject to afflictions of sin and death
Samaritanus		Christ	Christ, who made a journey from heaven to this world Mercy which cures
Oleum		Hope of mercy for the penitent	Penitence which purges
Vinum		Fear of punishment for the sinful	Christ proclaimed eternal life
Et alligavit vulnera		Christ restrained the sins which beset man by confuting them	Christ's flesh
Jumentum		Christ's flesh, bearing our sins on the cross	
Stabulum		Holy Church	Holy Church
Altera die		After the resurrection	First day of death begun in Adam. Second day of life begun in Christ
Duo denarii		Two Testaments	Two Testaments
Stabulario		Apostles	Holy Doctors

	pseudo-Hugh of St. Victor[6]	Hugh of St. Cher[7]	Denis the Carthusian[8]
Homo	Mankind	Adam or Mankind	Adam or Mankind after fall
Hierusalem	Heavenly city	Heavenly felicity	Terrestrial paradise and Kingdom of heaven
Hiericho	This world	Sorrows of this life	Mortality and instability of this life
Latrones	The ancient foe	Demons, passions or evil men	Demons

[6] *PL*. 175, 814-815.
[7] Vol. VI, fols. 194v-195v.
[8] Vol. XII, pp. 18a-21b.

Qui dispoliaverunt eum	Of the garment of immortality and innocence	Of the garment of virtue and spiritual riches	Of gifts of grace and spiritual power
Plagae	Original sin (orginalis culpae vitiis graviter vulneratum)	Injury and infirmity because of sin	4-fold result of original sin: malice, ignorance, infirmity, and concupiscence
Semivivus	Because the divine image and similitude in man has been corrupted but not effaced	Natural life retained; life of grace lost	Man's free will retained, though life of grace and charity lost
Sacerdos	The ancient Fathers who were powerless to aid the wounded man	The Law which came into the world through Moses	Aaron or priests of the law
Levita		Prophets	Moses, ministers of the temple, or prophets
Samaritanus	Christ descending from the Father into this world	Christ	Christ
Oleum	Preaching and consolation of Christ	Comfortable preaching or hope of eternal joy	Balm of consolation
Vinum	A stern rebuke	Fear of rebuke or heavenly joy	Comfort and earnest exhortation or a just rebuke for sins
Et alligavit vulnera		By the application of his Sacraments	Through an infusion of charity and grace
Jumentum	Christ's flesh which expiated our sins	Christ's flesh bearing the burden for our sins	Christ's body because he was the obedient servant
Stabulum	Holy Church	Holy Church	Holy Church
Altera die	After the redemption	Time before and after the resurrection	Time before and after the resurrection
Duo denarii	Full knowledge of 2 Testaments and Grace to preach	Full understanding of the two Testaments	Two Testaments
Stabulario	Prelates	The custodians of Holy Church: Prelates	Apostles or the Early Church

Thus the parable of the Good Samaritan is an allegory of the redemption of mankind. Personified in Adam, mankind foresakes the joys of paradise and is exiled to this world of sin, sorrow, and death. The patriarchs, prophets, and priests of the old dispensation travel along the same route, and though they are able to comprehend man's fallen state, they are powerless to help him. Finally Christ descends into the world and heals mankind by His grace.

Langland's paraphrase of the parable in lines 47-77 of Passus XVII is relatively exact and detailed. The man who has fallen among thieves lied naked and half-dead by the side of the road. Faith and Hope pass him by. The Samaritan, perceiving the wounded man's plight and great peril, goes to him, washes his wounds with oil and wine, binds his head, and carries him on his mule to an inn, where he makes provisions for the wounded man's care. Furthermore, the traditional interpretation as an allegory of man's redemption apparently underlies Langland's adaptation of the parable in a number of ways. For example, Langland's use of the parable of the Good Samaritan comes in close conjunction with the re-enactment in Passus XVIII of the final events of the Redemption. Again, the wounded traveller is seen as type of fallen mankind: "For went neuere wy in this worlde . thorw that wildernesse, / That he ne was robbed or rifled . rode he there or ȝede" (XVIII, 98-99). Then, of course, Christ is said to be *semblable* to the Samaritan at His triumphal entry into Jerusalem (XVIII, 10).

In addition, a few of the details of lines 46-77 are clarified by the traditional interpretation of the parable. For example, in *Piers* the wounded traveller is taken to a grange:

> Wyth wyn and with oyle . his woundes he wasshed,
> Enbawmed hum and bonde his hed . and in his lappe hym layde,
> And ladde hym so forth on lyard . to *lex-christi*, a graunge.
>
> (XVII, 69-71)

Before the sixteenth century, according to the *OED,* this term usually refers to a place for storing grain – in effect, a barn; or, more generally, it may refer to a farm as a whole. Langland's choice of the term *grange* may reflect commentaries on the *stabulum* of the parable, where the church is sometimes compared to a stable rather than to an inn. (Both meanings of the Latin *stabulum* are correct.) Hugh of St. Victor, for example, compares the church to a stable: just as beasts are cleansed in a stable, so sinners who have been leading bestial lives lay down their sins in holy church through confession and satisfaction.[9] Hugh of St. Cher calls the church a stable where the faithful are fed on the bread of God's word in the manger of Holy Scripture.[10] The important point is that Langland's use of the term *grange*, possibly derived from commentaries on the *stabulum* of the Parable of the Good Samaritan in which the term is universally glossed as the church, looks forward to the great configuration in Passus XIX of the building of the barn. On the other hand, Langland is careful to incorporate the second meaning of *stabulum* in the same passage: "Herberwed hym at an hostrye . and to the hostellere called, / And sayde, 'haue, kepe this man . til I come fro the Iustes' " (XVII, 73-74). The meaning of *stabulum* as an inn is not overlooked in the commentaries on the parable: for example, "Stabulum autem est Ecclesia praesens, ubi reficiuntur viatores de peregrinatione hac." [11] It is possible then that Langland's use of the term *graunge* followed by his use of the term *hostrye* may reflect the double meaning of *stabulum* – a double meaning recognized in standard commentary on the Parable of the Good Samaritan.

In emphasizing Langland's indebtedness to his scriptural source and its traditional interpretation, one should not overlook the minor changes incorporated by Langland. The Good Samaritan does not spend the night at the inn, as in the original parable. Instead, he makes the necessary arrangements at the inn for the care of the wounded traveller, and then he quickly departs for the joust in Jerusalem, pursued by Faith, Hope, and Will. Such an alteration, of course, contributes to the urgency of the narrative as the poem builds up to the climactic Passus XVIII. More-

---

9   *PL*. 175, 815.
10   Vol. VI, fol. 195v.
11   *PL*. 110, 450.

over, all the commentaries on *altera die* connect it with the time after the resurrection – an interpretation that would have precluded Langland's having the Good Samaritan spend the night, since the joust in Jerusalem has not yet occurred.

Langland also altered the scriptural account of the directions in which the various *personae* were proceeding. A man was going from Jerusalem to Jericho according to St. Luke, but in *Piers* the reader is not apprised of the traveller's direction. The priest and Levite were travelling the same route, i.e. Jerusalem to Jericho (Luke, X, 31-32), while in *Piers*, Faith, Hope, Will, and the Good Samaritan are proceeding towards Jerusalem:

> And as we wenten thus in the weye . wordyng togyderes,
> Thanne seye we a Samaritan . sittende on a mule,
> Rydynge ful rapely . the riʒt weye we ʒeden,
> Comynge fro a cuntre . that men called Iericho;
> To a Iustus in Iherusalem . he chaced awey faste.
>
> (XVII, 47–51)

The direction of the Good Samaritan is not given in the account in Luke; in the commentaries it is generally glossed as from heaven to earth. The primary explanation for these alterations is probably once again narrative urgency, building up to the climactic joust in Jerusalem which all the principals of Passus XVII will attend. At the same time, it is consistent with Langland's pilgrimage motif in a poem on the spiritual enlightenment of the human will, to have his characters tending towards Jerusalem with all its *nexus* of meanings, from earthly paradise to kingdom of God.

One of Langland's additions to the scriptural account of the Good Samaritan is significant. After the Samaritan has cleansed and bound the wounds of the traveller, Langland says, without precedent in Luke, "and in his lappe hym layde" (XVII, 70). In its poetic context, this mention of the Good Samaritan's lap contrasts effectively with the description at the end of Passus XVI (ll. 255-269) of Abraham's "lap". The contrast is the more effective because it is only Christ, typified in the Good Samaritan, who can free those in Abraham's lap from Satan's power:

Oute of the poukes pondfolde . no moynprise may vs fecche,
Tyl he come that I carpe of . Cryst is his name.
That shal delyure vs some daye . out of the deueles powere,
And bettere wedde for vs legge . than we ben alle worthy,
That is, lyf for lyf . or ligge thus euere
Lollynge in my lappe . tyl such a lorde vs fecche.

(XVI, 264–269)

A consideration of the traditional interpretations of the Parable of the Good Samaritan, however, does not adequately account for all the significant aspects of Langland's use of the parable. To appreciate fully the personification of charity in the Good Samaritan, one must give some attention to the connection made between Abraham-Faith-*sacerdos*, and Moses-*Spes*-Levita.

The identification of Abraham with faith is ultimately based on the scriptural account of his career in Genesis xv-xviii. This connection is reiterated several times in the New Testament: for example, Heb. xi, 17: "Fide obtulit Abraham Isaac, cum tentaretur." Again, Gal. iii, 7: "Cognoscite ergo, quia qui ex fide sunt, ii sunt filii Abrahae." The connection between Abraham and faith becomes a great staple of the exegetical tradition. For example, Hugh of St. Victor says: "Abraham dictus est prima via credendi, quia primum fides in eo enituit." [12] Hugh of St. Cher makes several references to Abraham as faith in commenting on the genealogy of Christ contained in the first chapter of Matthew. For example: "Abraham, qui est fides, et via credendi"; or, "Per Abraham fides, qui dicitur prima via credendi, non quod primas crediderit, vel quod fidem unius Dei solus habuerit, imo Noe ante dilivium." [13] The identification between faith and Abraham is treated fully by Robertson and Huppé. [14] The visit of the three angels to Abraham (Gen. xviii, 1-2) alluded to by Langland (XVI, 225-229) signifies Abraham's faith in the Trinity; such a belief in the Trinity is the basis of faith in the Athanasian Creed. Abraham's faith is further attested by his willingness to sacrifice Isaac and by the circumcision of himself and his household.

While the connection between Abraham and faith looms large

[12] *PL*. 175, 886.
[13] Vol. VI, fols. 3r-4r.
[14] Pp. 198-203.

in the exegetical tradition, considerable investigation has un-
covered no commentary on the Parable of the Good Samaritan
in which the *sarcedos* is explicitly identified with Abraham. However, the priest of the parable is often enough taken as a type of
the patriarchs (see table above), and a specific identification with
Abraham, the first and greatest patriarch, would represent an
obvious development of the standard interpretation of *sacerdos*.
Moreover, Abraham is referred to as *sacerdos* in contexts other
than that of the Parable of the Good Samaritan.[15]

In contrast, Moses is often specifically connected with the
Parable of the Good Samaritan. In its scriptural context, the
parable itself is connected with the summary of the Mosaic law
which opens Passus XVII (lines 9-13). Moreover, from the table
above it will be seen that several of the commentators associate
Moses with either the priest or the Levite; Denis the Carthusian
glosses the Levite of the parable as Moses.[16] Such an association
is to be expected in view of the fact that Moses is the foremost
of the tribe of Levi. In addition, just as the priest of the parable
is often connected with the patriarchs, so the Levite is connected
with the prophets; an obvious development of such an interpretation would be a connection with Moses, the greatest of Old Testament prophets.

A specific connection between Moses and the Levite of the
Parable of the Good Samaritan is derived from the exegetical
tradition more transparently than the identification between
Abraham and the priest. However, the connection between Moses
and hope is less obvious than the connection between Abraham
and faith. The aptness of the comparison of Moses to hope re-
sides, I think, in the nature of the tablets of the law exhibited by
Spes to Will. The law, according to orthodox medieval Christianity, must be fulfilled by good works; and good works nourish the
virtue of hope. The concept, derived from St. Augustine, that good

---

[15] See, for example, Hugh of St. Cher, Vol. VI, fol. 4r, where Abraham is
called *sacerdos* because he sacrificed the ram in place of his own son. See
also Robertson and Huppé, pp. 201-202.
[16] Moses is also associated with the episode of the priest and the Levite
in stained-glass representations of the parable. See, for example, Émile
Mâle, *L'art religieux du XIIᵉ Siècle en France* (Paris, 1924), pp. 196-197.

works are the reasonable basis for hope, became one of the governing precepts of medieval Christianity. Sister Rose Bernard Donna [17] cites passage after passage from *Piers* where the concept is stated or implied. Standard commentary of the late Middle Ages also attests to the continued vitality of the concept. For example, Hugh of St. Cher, commenting on Ps. iv, 6, defines hope: "Spes est certa expectatio futurae beatitudinis, *ex meritis proveniens* [italics mine]." [18] Denis the Carthusian reiterates this precept several times: "Qui autem sine operibus virtutem sperat salvari inaniter sperat." [19] In short, the Middle Ages regarded good works as nourishing the virtue of hope, just as evil actions nourish its antithesis, despair.[20] In addition, there is a scriptural connection between hope and the law. Heb. vii, 19 reads: "Nihil enim ad perfectionem adduxit lex. Introductio vero melioris spei, per quam proximamus ad Deum." According to Hugh of St. Cher, the hope brought in by the Old Law was the expectation of a better law, the Law of Christ, whose observance would confer eternal glory, as opposed to the Old Law, whose observance conferred hope, but not salvation.[21]

This passage from the epistle to the Hebrews, then, along with its commentary, not only relates the virtue of hope to the Law of Moses, but also relates the Old Law of Moses to the New Law of Christ. This great medieval commonplace, that the Old Law was fulfilled or perfected in the New Law, also underlies the traditional interpretation of the Parable of the Good Samaritan. The *Glossa Ordinaria* connects the priest of the parable with the insufficiency of the Old Law to restore mankind to a state of grace.[22] The priest of the parable is also identified by Hugh of St. Cher

---

[17] *Despair and Hope: A Study in Langland and Augustine* (Washington, 1948), pp. 75-78.
[18] Vol. II, fol. 9v.
[19] Vol. XIV, p. 413a; Vol. VI, p. 359b. On Ps. xxxi, 10, and Ps. xc, 1, respectively.
[20] Since the medieval psychology of hope is peripheral to a study of charity imagery, the above remarks have been necessarily brief and overly simple.
[21] Vol. VI, fol. 253v.
[22] *PL*. 114, 286: "Sacerdos Dei legem annuntiat: descendit quidem lex per Moysen in mundum, et nullam sanitatem contulit hujusmodi."

with the law, "quae descendit in mundum per Moysen"; though he, the law, can make known the sins and wounds of mankind, he does not cure them.[23] The inefficacy of the Old Law unfulfilled by the New Law of Christ is variously expressed in the commentaries. Hugh of St. Cher, commenting on the eight chapter of Hebrews, echoes his own pronouncement on the priest of the parable: "Lex enim morbum ostendebat, sed non sanabat." [24] Hugh of St. Victor says that what Moses taught he himself was unable to fulfill – that is, without God's grace perfect obedience to the law of love is impossible – while Christ was able to practice what He taught.[25] Grace is emphasized by Denis the Carthusian in a comment on Rom. viii, 2, as a vital element lacking under the Old Law; [26] he asserts that it is not the Law of Moses but the Law of Christ which justifies mankind through grace.[27]

Several details of Passus XVII are illumined by the concept of the Old Law of Moses perfected or completed in the New Law of Christ. One of these is the name given by Langland to the grange signifying the Church, where the Good Samaritan harbors the wounded man – lex-christi (XVII, 71). Another is the statement by Spes that his "maundement" has not been sealed: " 'Is it asseled?' I seyd . 'may men se thi lettres?' / 'Nay,' he sayde, 'I seke hym . that hath the sele to kepe' " (XVII, 4-5). Among various meanings of seal, the OED records: "A final addition which completes and secures" (Vol. IX, p. 323c), with examples as early as ca. 1320. Both of these details from Piers maintain the traditional connection between the Parable of the Good Samaritan and the insufficiency of the Old Law.

[23] Vol. VI, fol. 195r.
[24] Vol. VI, fol. 253r.
[25] PL. 175, 783: "Lex per Moysen data est; gratia et veritas per Jesum Christum (John i, 17) quia quod Moyses docuit, ipse adimplere nequaquam potuit; unde dedit quod ipso facere non potuit; sed Jesus Christus quod docuit, hoc ipsum etiam opere adimplevit."
[26] Vol. II, p. 721b: "Lex ergo nova veterem implet, quia quod ei defuit, addit, videlicet perfectionis consilis gratiam quoque praebens ex merito passionis Christi, qua homo potens efficitus implere quae praecipiuntur."
[27] Vol. XIII, pp. 273b-274a: "Lex etenim Christi virtute sacramentorum suorum gratiam confert, sicque justificat, non autem lex Moysis. – Ea vero quae his dicuntur de insufficientia legis scriptae et efficacia legis novae, in epistola ad Romanos plenius subtiliusque conscriptae atque tractata sunt."

Moreover, there is considerable evidence that this traditional connection is further elaborated by Langland. Ingenius schemes for dividing historical time into great epochs or world ages were devised in the Middle Ages. One of the more common of these is a threefold division into time "ante legem, sub lege, in gratia".[28] This same division is also expressed as the time of natural law from Adam to Moses, the time of scriptural law from Moses to Christ, and the time of grace or of evangelical law from Christ to the end of the world.[29] Sometimes this scheme is used to divide mankind into three great classes.[30] In particular, the patriarchs are thought of as dominating the period of the natural law, while the prophets dominated the period of the scriptural law.[31] Of the patriarchs, Abraham is the figure most often cited in connection with the period of the natural law.[32] In his tract *De Sacramentis,* where a basic structural device is the threefold division of the law, Hugh of St Victor juxtaposes the natural law, faith, and Abraham.[33] Moses, the greatest of the prophets, as well as the law-giver, would be the obvious type of mankind under the scriptural law. This traditional distinction between the natural and the scriptural law certainly underlies Will's question: "What neded it thanne . a newe lawe to bigynne, / Sith the fyrst sufficeth . to sauacioun and to blisse?" (XVII, 30-31). It is unmistakable from the context of these lines that the contrast is between the teachings of Abraham and Moses, not between the Old Law of

28 Hugh of St. Cher, Vol. II, fol. 173v; Vol. III, fol. 151v.
29 Hugh of St. Victor, *PL.* 176, 32.
30 *Ibid.:* "Similiter tria sunt genera hominum; id est homincs naturalis legis dici possunt qui sola naturali ratione vitam suam dirigunt. . . . Homines scriptae legis sunt ii qui exteriobus praeceptis ad bene vivendum informantur. Homines gratiae sunt ii qui per aspirationem Spiritus Sancti afflati et illuminantur ut bonum quod faciendum est agnoscant, et inflammantur ut diligant, et corroborantur ut perficiant."
31 Godefrid of Admont, *PL.* 174, 34.
32 Hugh of St. Cher, Vol. VI, fol. 3r. Also, Hugh of St. Victor, *PL.* 176, 347.
33 *PL.* 176, 347: "Primum illud saeculum sub lege naturali, quasi in confusione quadam transierat; et qui in eo fideles exstiterant, quasi pauca quaedam grana in humano genere dispersa, et ab invicem discreta, sola intus fide unita fuerant. . . . Vocatus est Abraham unus ex multis; unitas principium unionis, ut ad sinum illus colligerentur quicumque post illum fide illi et devotione jungerentur."

Moses and the New Law of Christ. In addition, Langland's identification of *sacerdos* of the Parable of the Good Samaritan with
Abraham is not a commonplace of the exegetical tradition, while
the association of Abraham with the time of natural law is. It
seems a likely possibility then that it was Langland's intention for
Abraham to typify the faithful men of the epoch governed by
natural law, and Moses, men of the second epoch, hopeful because of the revelation of scriptural law. Within this framework,
the Good Samaritan, basically personifying charity, becomes, of
course, a type of the New Law of love. At least three other traditional patterns or frames of reference underlie the progression
from Abraham-faith and Moses-hope to Good Samaritan. The
first of these has to do with the perfection of the virtues of faith
and hope in the virtue of charity; the second, with the salvation
in Christ of the just of the Old Testament; the third, with the
fulfillment of faith and works in love.

Rom. xiii, 10, "Plentitudo ergo legis est dilectio", is the most
concise scriptural statement of the pattern already proposed –
that of the Old Law fulfilled in the New. However, in his commentary, Hugh of St. Cher relates this verse to the operation and
perfection of all the virtues, especially faith.[34] Though expressed
negatively, a similar concept of the relative imperfection of faith
and hope by themselves underlies Hugh's comment on I Cor. xiii,
10: "Cum autem venerit quod perfectum est, evacuabitur quod
ex parte est." [35] True faith is vivified by charity, and just as life
is recognized by movement, so the life of faith is recognized by

---

[34]   Vol. VII, fol. 65v: "Triplex, quia movet, et incitat alias virtutes ad
opera. *Galat.* V, Fides, quae per charitatem operatur, quia opus fidei est
credere, et ubi amor, ibi oculus. Matth. VI, Ubi est thesaurus tuus, ibi cor
tuum; idest oculus mentis credendo: ad quod facit illus: *trahit sua quemque
voluptas.* Et maxima voluptas est in charitate, et ideo trahit caeteras virtutis
ad operandum pro dilecto. Secunda ratio est, *quia charitatis consummat
inchoata ab aliis virtutibus* . . . [italics mine]. Dilectio enim facit perseve-
rare in motu incipto ab aliis virtutibus. Tertia ratio est, quia opera aliarum
virtutum sine ea vana sunt, et vacua.
[35]   Vol. VII, fol. 110v: "Quaedam virtutes ex propria natura imperfectio-
nem habent; ut fides ex propria natura sua habet quod sit de eo quod non
videtur; et spes similiter quia quod videt quis quid sperat? et ideo evacua-
buntur et ex parte dicuntur. Charitas autem est tum de eo quod videt, tum
de eo quod non videt, et ei accidit quod sit de eo quod non videt, quod

charitable works.[36] Hope, as pointed out above, is nourished in the individual Christian by his awareness of a practicing spirit of love manifested in his own life in his good deeds. Nor can the Christian hope for God's mercy without a prior awareness of God's love. In terms of medieval psychology, one would only hope for that which he has first loved. Within the narrative framework of Passus XVII, the hope of salvation is futile until the joust in Jerusalem. After this climactic event, however, faith and hope will be infused with a new power, so that they can lead men to salvation:

"Haue hem excused", quod he . "her help may litel auaille;
May no medcyn on molde . the man to hele brynge,
Neither Feith ne fyn Hope . so festred ben his woundis,
With-out the blode of a barn . borne of a mayde.
. . . .
For went neuere wy in this worlde . thorw that wildernesse,
That he ne was robbed or ritled . rode he thero or jede,
. . . .
For outlawes in the wode . and vnder banke lotyeth,
And may vch man se . and gode merke take,
. . . .
Ac ar this day thre dayes . I dar vndertaken,
That he worth fettred, that feloune . fast with cheynes,
And neure eft greue grome . that goth this ilke gate;
    O mors, ero mors tua, etc.,
And thanne shal Feith be forester here . and in this fritth
    walke,
And kennen out commune men . that knoweth nou3te the contre,
Which is the weye that ich went . and wherforth to Iherasulem.
And Hope the hostelleres man shal be . there the man lith an
    helynge;
And alle that fieble and faynt be . that Faith may nou3t teche,
Hope shal lede hem forth with lone . as his lettre telleth.
                    (XVII, 90–93, 98–99, 102–103, 109–117)

Not only is the Old Law fulfilled in the New and the virtues of faith and hope vitalized by charity, but the historical Abraham and Moses, and all the just men of the Old Testament, are saved

---

habet a fide: et ideo licet quantum ad hoc sit evacuanda, quia tamen illud ei accidit, non debet dici evacuari, nec ex parte posita."
[36] Hugh of St. Cher, Vol. I, fol. 36r.

by the unbounded love of Christ.[37] Thus, Abraham is seeking the
Christ: "I seke after a segge . that I seigh ones, / A ful bolde
bacheler . I knewe hym by his blasen" (XVI, 178-179); again, in
the brief description of limbo which concludes Passus XVI:

> Oute of the poukes pondfolde . no meynprise may vs fecche
> Tyl he come that I carpe of . Cryst is his name,
> That shal delyure vs some daye . out of the deueles powere,
> And bettere wedde for vs legge . than we ben all worthy,
> That is, lyf for lyf . or ligge thus euere.

(XVI, 264–268)

Spes is also looking for the Christ-knight: " 'I am *Spes*,' quod
he, 'a spye . and spire after a kny3te' " (XVII, 1). This pattern
is supported by standard commentary on the *altera die* of the
parable; for example, Honorius of Autun summarizes the lot of
mankind under the old dispensation:

> Altera die protulit duos denarios. Una dies erat mortis, altera vitae.
> Dies mortis coepit ab Adam, in quo omnes moriuntur. Dies vitae in-
> choavit a Christo, in quos omnes vivificabuntur. Ante Christi resur-
> rectionem omnes homines ad mortem tendebant; post suam resurrec-
> tionem omnes fideles ad vitam surgebant.[38]

Apparently both Abraham and *Spes* recognize in the Good Samaritan the person they are seeking, since they hastily pursue
him after he has revealed himself by healing the wounds of mankind (XVII, 80-82).

Finally, the traditional connection already alluded to between
spes and good works suggests that faith and works alone are in-
sufficient for salvation. In other words, man's best efforts could
not earn him salvation, which can only result from the free gift
of God's grace brought to man in the person of Christ, typified
in the Good Samaritan (see table on pp. 75-77).

Thus at least four thematic patterns may be seen to underlie
the figurative progression in *Piers* from Abraham-Faith and
Moses-*Spes* to the Good Samaritan: the fulfillment of the Old
Law in the New; the perfection and operation of faith and hope

---

[37]   See, for example, Hugh of St. Cher, Vol. VI, fol. 3ᵛ; and Denis the
Carthusian, Vol. II, p. 721b.
[38]   *PL.* 172, 1060.

through the virtue of charity; the salvation of the just men of the
old dispensation through the supreme act of charity, Christ's
sacrificial offering of himself; and, finally, the salvation of mankind, not through his own efforts, but by the unearned gift of
divine grace. The coalescing of these patterns in Passus XVII is
so complete that they do not submit to analysis according to the
four levels of biblical exegesis, or to any other scheme that the
reader may wish to resort to; the effect is analogous to Spencer's
in the early books of the *Faerie Queene*; in one passage one allegorical pattern rises to the surface; in a later passage, another.
This does not mean, however, that they were not an integral part
of the organic construction of Passus XVII for both Langland
and his medieval audience. Such patterns are the stock-in-trade
of the medieval Christian culture which produced *Piers,* and it is
hoped that enough details from the poem itself have been adduced
to support their presence in *Piers.* While the proposed thematic
patterns seem to be coalesced rather than stratified in the poem,
they do culminate in the figure of the Good Samaritan obviously
personifying charity in the poem, and inescapably typifying
Christ for the medieval Christian, certainly aware of the standard interpretations of well-known parables. Charity fulfills the
law and perfects all other virtues; and Christ brings the unearned
gift of salvation to all mankind, whether under the old or the new
dispensation. By generalizing a traditional type of Christ into a
personification of charity as well, Langland sustains and concludes the various patterns proposed for the figurative progression
of the latter part of Passus XVI and of Passus XVII. At the same
time, the poet maintains and emphasizes the traditional identification of the Good Samaritan with Christ. The Samaritan, riding
the mule *Caro* borrowed from mankind (see table on pp. 75-77),
is on his way to Jerusalem for the joust with Satan; in Passus XVII,
line 10, Christ, entering Jerusalem, is said to be *semblable* to the
Good Samaritan.

Matter traditionally connected with the Parable of the Good
Samaritan also clarifies to some degree a rather obscure statement of the Samaritan concerning the promised vivifying and
perfecting of faith and hope. The Samaritan promises Will that

in three days Satan will be bound in chains, and death vanquished; and that thereupon Faith and Hope will be enabled to act effectively on behalf of mankind, instead of hastening by on the other side of the road. Will is then told that Hope will continue to serve as comforter and physician until the Good Samaritan has a cure for all the sick, when he will return and comfort all the sick who crave, covet, or cry after his cure:

> And alle that fieble and faynt be . that Faith may nou3t teche,
> Hope shal lede hem forth with loue . as his lettre telleth,
> And come a3ein bi this contree . and confort alle syke
> Tyl I haue salue for all syke . and thanne shal I retourne,
> And hostel hem and hele . thorw holecherche bileue,
> That craueth it or coueiteth it . and cryeth there-after.
>
> (XVII, 116–121)

The crux of this passage: "What is the nature of this second coming, and what is the function of this reference in the poem?"

The liturgical connections of the Parable of the Good Samaritan are with the season of Pentecost. It is contained in the gospel for the twelfth Sunday after Pentecost; it is the text of a sermon for the thirteenth Sunday after Pentecost in the *Speculum Ecclesiae* of Honorius of Autun; [39] and it is the text of a sermon by St. Bonaventura [40] for the twelfth Sunday after Pentecost. This association with Pentecost is also found in the commentaries on the Parable, where the two denarii given to the Innkeeper by the Good Samaritan are glossed as the understanding of Scripture and the ability to preach, which came upon the Apostles at Pentecost (see table on pp. 75-77). In addition to this traditional association with the season of Pentecost, the parable is also connected with the second coming of Christ in judgement, usually in glossing "cum rediero" of Luke x, 35; [41] and the repayment promised to the inkeeper upon the Good Samaritan's return is glossed as the final reward of worthy pastors. [42] May these traditional con-

---

[39]   *PL*. 172, 1059-1061.
[40]   Vol. IX, pp. 398a-401b.
[41]   In addition, *altera die* of the parable is always glossed *post resurrectionem* (see table on pp. 75-77).
[42]   See, for example, Rabanus Maurus, *PL*. 110, 450; Honorius of Autun, *Speculum Ecclesiae, PL*. 172, 1061; Hugh of St. Victor, *PL*. 175, 815.

nections of the parable either with Pentecost or with the second coming of Christ in judgement illumine the obscure passage from Langland under examination?

The content of the lines suggests that the reference is not to the coming of the Holy Ghost at Pentecost, since the advent referred to by Langland apparently occurs after the founding of the church: Hope is called the hosteler's man, and the hosteler or innkeeper is traditionally glossed as the apostolic succession; and there is a further reference in line 118 to "holicherche bileue". However, the traditional connection of the Parable of the Good Samaritan with Pentecost may survive in *Piers* in the choice of one word, *confort* (XVII, 120), echoing the promise of the *paraclete,* the comforter, in John xiv, 16, 26. If the fourteenth chapter of St. John underlies these few lines of *Piers* as a corollary to the traditional associations of the Parable of the Good Samaritan with Pentecost, then further references to a second coming of Christ, in addition to those to be derived from commentary on the parable itself, would present themselves. John xiv, 18 reads: "Non relinquam orphanos: veniam ad vos." Denis the Carthusian glosses: "Post resurrectionem, per sensibilem apparitionem, spiritualem consolationem, internamque visitationem." [43] Of Christ's promise recorded in John xiv, 28, "Vado, et venio ad vos", Hugh of St. Cher says: "Idest ad vestram consolationem veniam ad vos: ideo non timeatis de imminente tribulatione: quia veniam in auxilium, et solatium." [44]

As suggested by the glosses on John xiv already cited, medieval exegetes distinguish various symbolic advents of Christ. They include the indwelling spirit of Christ in the individual Christian and the coming of Christ to the individual Christian in death.[45] While overtones of such symoblic "comings" may inform Langland's reference, his basic allusion is, I think, to the second coming in judgement. The difficulty with such an interpretation is,

[43] Vol. XII, p. 536b.
[44] Vol. VI, fol. 374r.
[45] For a discussion of these and other symbolic "comings" of Christ, see Henri de Lubac, S.J., *Exégèse Médiévale* (Paris, 1959), Vol. II, pp. 621-626.

of course, the apparently heretical allusion to universal salvation: "Tyl I haue salue for alle syke . and thanne shal I retourne ... and confort alle syke" (XVII, 119-120). There are several aspects to the answer to this difficulty. In the first place, the immediately following line makes it clear that the allusion is not to universal salvation in the sense that unrepentant sinners, willy nilly, are promised salvation; in fact, it is the sick who "crave, covet, and cry after" the Good Samaritan's cure who will receive this benefit. In the second place, the narrative structure of *Piers* demands that the "salve" universally available, not universally received, be characterized as a future blessing: the joust at Jerusalem has not as yet taken place. In the third place, and it is here that the traditional associations of the Parable of the Good Samaritan with the second coming are especially significant, the joust at Jerusalem will not immediately procure the final restoration of mankind; the struggle with Antichrist continues in this world. But, at the second coming, the consummation of the ages, the ultimate and eternal restoration of the faithful will take place, and the forces of Antichrist will be eternally defeated. In the meantime, it is the responsibility of the church and her priests to continue the work begun by Christ of redeeming the world:

> And Hope the hostelleres man shal be . there the man lith an
>   helynge;
> And alle that fieble and faynt be . that Faith may nouȝt teche,
> Hope shal lede hem forth with loue . as his lettre telleth,
> And hostel hem and hele . thorw holicherche bileue,
> Tyl I haue salue for alle syke.
>
> (XVII, 115–119)

Passus XIX and XX make it clear that Langland was realistic about the nature of man in this world even after the eternal battle has been won in Jerusalem. However, he employs the traditional association of the Parable of the Good Samaritan with the second coming of Christ to give Will as well as his reader a rare glimpse of the final restoration to take place at the consummation of all things.

In the above paragraphs the attempt has been made to show the extent to which the traditional interpretation of the Parable of the Good Samaritan informs portions of Passus XVII. This influence ranges from the choice of individual words such as *grange*, to the determining of significant thematic patterns such as the fulfillment of the Old Law in the New. Moreover, evaluation of certain aspects of the traditional interpretation of the parable helps to clarify a rather obscure reference to another coming of the Good Samaritan. As Langland has used the figure of the Good Samaritan, he is both a personification of charity and a type of Christ. In fulfilling this dual function, the figure of the Good Samaritan helps the poet sustain a complexity of meaning for Passus XVII.

V

CONCLUSION

I have now completed a discussion of those sections of *Piers* where an awareness of the traditional context of the imagery of charity seems essential for a full realization of what the poem has to communicate. A summary of the preceding chapters is now in order.

Chapter I deals with Lady Holy Church's characterization of charity, with emphasis on lines 146-162 of Passus I. Love as the *triacle* of heaven is seen to be an overt reference to standard commentary on Num. xxi, 5-9 – commentary which discusses the *therica* derived from the brazen serpent. Other references to matter from the Old Testament (the creative acts and the career of Moses), recalling manifestations of charity under the old dispensation, terminate in the figure of the plant of peace. The latter is organically related to the ensuing figure: heavenly love which falls to earth and eats of the earth to become fully incarnate. This figure is inevitably associated with a traditional prefiguration of the Incarnation of Christ – the figure of the dew on the fleece of Gedeon – and with commentary on scriptural passages related to this prefiguration, especially passages in Isaiah and in the psalms. Disembodied love, heavy with the desire to become incarnate, becomes, paradoxically, so light and piercing after its incarnation that it can penetrate the armor of the Devil and the walls of sin. Thus love leads God's people back to Him and acts at the same time as a mediator between God and His people; in addition, divine love judges and punishes. Finally, love, ordained by power, has its source in the wellspring of the heart. Further examination of these latter images suggests that while their immediate reference is to various aspects of charity, they are also related to or derived from imagery primarily associated with Christ. Other imagery from Lady Holy Church's speech is also dealt with in Chapter I, notably the overt reference in lines 186-187 to the Parable of the Wise and the Foolish Virgins.

Chapter II is an extended treatment of Patience's riddle (Passus XIII, lines 135-156). The progression *disce, doce, dilige*, not only asserts the scholastic concept of the interdependence of wisdom and love, but as this progression is elaborated by Patience, it also suggests a gradual *distentio charitatis*. The use of the image of the burning coals is seen to accord with standard commentary on Prov. xxv, 21-22 and on Rom. xii, 20. Though my solution of the riddle itself resists an adequate summary, let us review its major points. First of all, the terms of the riddle must be understood. *Kynde loue* is taken to be unobstructed and unselfish love characteristic of God. Such love, desiring nothing material, does "covet" self-expression – the consummate expression of such love having been the Word made flesh. The "half lamp line" is seen to be a reference to Ps. iv, 7, which, according to its "transitive" interpretation by medieval commentators, includes references to both the creation and the redemption of the world. The "sign of the Saturday" and the "wit of the Wednesday of the next week" are seen to refer once again to the interdependence of love and wisdom, especially as these two Christian goals are joined together in the person of Christ and endorsed in His resurrection.

Chapter III deals with one of the central images in *Piers* – that of the tree of charity. This image is shown to be basically eclectic, consisting of various elements derived from a number of trees in the Christian tradition, elements which are synthesized by the poet. Of these trees, the Tree of Life or the Cross, is especially significant. However, the Tree of Jesse, the Tree of Virtues, and trees showing the descent of man – especially those in which Adam's progeny is classified according to the three grades of chastity – also help to shape Langland's image. Moreover, in synthesizing several figurative trees, Langland is again acting in accordance with the Christian tradition, since medieval exegetes themselves often conflate these figures.

Chapter IV deals with the personification of charity as the Good Samaritan, in Passus XVII. This chapter suggests that in this extensive and detailed use of his scriptural source, Langland is taking for granted the standard medieval interpretation of the parable as an allegory of Christ's redemption of the world; it also shows that several of the details of Passus XVII were shaped, in part at least, either by the standard interpretation of the parable or by its liturgical context. A notable example is the reference in line 120 to a second coming. In addition, a few significant changes are wrought by Langland in the scriptural account of the Good Samaritan, primarily for the sake of allegorical consistency or narrative effectiveness. Furthermore, various patterns of allegory result fom the progression Abraham/Faith, Moses/Hope, and Good Samaritan/Charity. They include the salvation of the Just of the Old Testament through Christ; the fulfillment of natural and scriptural law in the New Law of love; the perfection of the other theological virtues in charity; and the ultimate inefficacy of any means, other than divine grace, to lead mankind to God.

It now remains to draw some of the general conclusions which are implicit in the material summarized above. Although the new findings of such a study as this one tend to emerge in the individual chapters themselves, my findings can be used to facilitate the further interpretation of the poem by indicating the method characteristic of Langland's use of traditional imagery of charity – a method whereby both the individual configurations and the overall development of the imagery are clearly patterned. Secondly, and apart from the context of the poem itself, a few more general conclusions are indicated about the ways in which Langland uses exegetical imagery.

A consistent pattern or principle of construction is observable in the various configurations of charity examined in the preceding chapters. Basically, Langland lifts each detail of a pattern of imagery from some traditional source, often but not always Christian; he then combines these details into a unique pattern with a force and validity of its own. At the same time, each detail of the pattern of imagery evokes something of its own traditional source, so that by allusion and association each pattern of imagery is supported by a variety of traditional material. Thus, at his best, the poet succeeds in holding a number of disparate elements of imagery in a state of suspension. At the same time, the pull of the traditional sources of each element or fragment sets up a ten sion which is responsible, at least in part, for the tremendous vitality of Langland's configurations. To put it another way, Langland takes several traditional patterns of imagery, shatters each, selects certain fragments, and assembles a new pattern. At the same time, each element of the new pattern is inevitably attracted toward its old pattern. For example, one expects to find the image of treacle either in a pattern of images associated with the Passion or in a pattern which includes the brazen serpent, fiery snakes, the "prop", the murmurings of the Hebrews, etc. Instead, it is found in a pattern which includes the Creation, the law of Moses, the Incarnation, the walls and armor of sin and the Devil, and the town mayor as leader, mediator, and judge of his people. Such a pattern yields a figurative exposition which is, at the same time, highly compressed yet highly evocative. In addition, there is usually a controlling image or idea which integrates and unifies the new pattern of imagery. In the pattern being cited, continuous reference to imagery primarily associated with Christ seems to fulfill this function.

A similar principle of construction can be detected in the imagery of Patience's speech, where material traditionally associated with the creation and the re-creation of the world is joined to material traditionally associated with medieval theories of grammar and unified by the traditional interdependence of wisdom and love. Similarly, the vision of the tree of charity consists of a number of figurative details derived from several trees of the Christian tradition – details which bear their own weight of allusion but which, at the same time, are controlled and synthesized through the use of the emblematic tree. Finally, the imagery of Passus XVII, derived from a number of traditional Christian sources, is unified by its traditional associations with the Parable of the Good Samaritan. Thus, the Christian tradition not only provides most of the elements of Langland's patterns of charity imagery, but also the unifying principle of these patterns.

Let us now consider the possibility of still broader patterns in the over-all development of the imagery of charity. In Passus I, Lady Holy Church gives a highly figurative exposition of charity. After Passus I, the poem is largely governed by the motif of the quest. Though the object of this quest appears under various guises, it is generally conceded to be the great Christian goal of truth and love – actually twin goals, largely inseparable within Langland's frame of reference: truth teaches the Christian the nature of love (I, 146); truth is caught up in a chain of charity (V, 615-616); learning and teaching will reveal charity (the partial solution to Patience's riddle). If the search for charity is a primary aspect of Will's quest, then the motif of the quest might be expected to govern Langland's use of the imagery of charity. This study suggests that such is the case.

As has already been noted, Lady Holy Church's characterization of charity is largely descriptive or expository. For example, charity is treacle or salve for sin. Charity motivated the creative acts, and it is the summation of the Mosaic law. From charity divine peace springs like a plant, etc. Other figures of charity appearing in Lady Holy Church's speech reflect the individual Christian's obligation to charity: for example, the figure in which chastity without charity is compared to a lamp without a light and faith without works (I, 183-187). After this preliminary description of charity and its central position in the life of the Christian, Will seeks charity actualized in the human condition. In this quest Will is dismayed by his many experiences, some of them disillusioning. However, in a timely encounter in Passus XIII, Will is given further instruction in charity by Clergy and Patience (lines 119-171), assuring Will that the patient conquer. This instruction differs from that of Lady Holy Church in that Patience's lesson is more immediately concerned with the operation of charity in human affairs: the epitome of charity is love for one's enemies, and Will is enjoined to overcome his enemy with charity. However, there is another obvious difference between the two lessons in charity. Will's instruction by Lady Holy Church, though fraught with evocative imagery, is straightforward and obvious compared to the conclusion of Patience's lesson. That is, it is according to the precept "Love thine enemies" that the practicing Christian ought to regulate his affairs among men; however, while this precept is easy enough to mouth, it is difficult to practice. Therefore, the difficulties and complexities of the process whereby one is able to cast coals of charity upon his enemy, are suggested in the obscurity of Patience's riddle.

A cryptic riddle cannot settle Will's doubts about the nature of the good life, so that at the beginning of Passus XV he seizes the opportunity to question Anima about charity. Throughout the remainder of Passus XV Anima attempts to describe charity for Will, relying primarily on the Pauline epistles. When Will, at the beginning of Passus XVI, is still dissatisfied, all Anima can do is resort to the conventional device of a schematized tree of which the root is mercy, the trunk is pity, the leaves are faithful words, the blossoms are kind speech and gentle looks, and the fruit is charity. However, as a result Will has his first direct experience with charity in the form of a contemplative vision – which is actually an inspired extension of the figure of the tree described by Anima – culminating in the figure of the three grades of chastity as emblematical of the various possible manifestations of charity.

When Will awakes from the vision, the quest for charity continues, merged now with the quest for Piers, the lord of the tree of charity. Finally in Passus XVII, having had the doctrine of charity expounded by the church, having learned that in human terms any attempt to discover the means of loving one's enemies ends in the perplexity of a riddle, having had his purpose strengthened by a vision of charity, Will at last meets charity face to face,[1]

---

1   In this connection, it should be noted that the imagery of Passus XVII is "domesticated" to a greater degree than is observable in Will's other experiences with charity. For example, Abraham is a herald and Moses is

personified as the Good Samaritan. Moreover, in his role as a type of Christ, and merged with Piers, the Good Samaritan can defeat on man's behalf the forces of sin and death. In Passus XVIII, then, the quest is over: having seen charity fully manifested, the Christian is able to fulfill the law of love through the power of his champion, the knight of charity. However, Will's full and immediate experience with charity is short-lived; for though charity's battle is won eternally, temporally the struggle with Antichrist and the quest for Piers go on. The aged and despairing Will of Passus XX is once again advised to "learn to love" (line 207).

If the progression from exposition and instruction to visionary apprehension and direct experience culminates in the personification of charity as the Good Samaritan, a universal type of Christ, then the traditional associations with Christ, informing much of the earlier imagery of charity, no longer seem circumstantial. If the culminating image of charity is to typify Christ, a well-wrought pattern of imagery is indicated by the fact that most of the other images of charity are traditionally associated with Christ. Prominent examples of such imagery in *Piers* are the treacle, incarnate love, the needle, the mediator, the re-creation, and the tree of life. In this connection it is particularly significant, I think, that after Will has learned the doctrine of charity from the church, his search for the charitable life leads first of all to Patience's riddle – a riddle whose solution is bound up with the "middle of the moon", Christ's resurrection. Is it stretching a point to see in Passus XVII and XVIII, where the events surrounding the resurrection are re-enacted, and expanded, literal statement of all that is cryptically implied in Patience's riddle? If not, it would seem that the over-all development of the imagery of charity in *Piers* is carefully patterned.

Let us now consider the conclusions indicated by this study about Langland's use of exegetical imagery in general. The preceding study indicates that he uses exegetical imagery in at least

---

a "spy"; there are references to a grange, to woods filled with robbers, and to a forester.

three different ways, some perhaps more subtle than others. First, he invokes the traditional associations of scripturally derived imagery: for example, the needle, derived from Luke xviii, 25; the walls, derived from Cant. ii, 9; the lamp without a light, derived from the Parable of the Wise and the Foolish Virgins; the burning coals, derived from Prov. xxv, 21-22 and Rom. xii, 20; the figure of the Good Samaritan, derived from the parable in Luke. In every case, it is not the scriptural source which is significant in appreciating and understanding Langland's image, but, rather, the traditional interpretation of the source.

Secondly, Langland sometimes transposes an image directly from the exegetical tradition into his poem. For example, the image of the treacle is derived immediately from commentary rather than from Scripture. Likewise, though medieval theories of grammar must also be invoked, standard commentary on Ps. iv, 7 is one of the sources of Patience's riddle, not to mention the extension of the hexameral tradition which includes the "week" of the re-creation.

Finally, Langland will take an image whose immediate source is neither Scripture nor commentary and weight it with exegetical overtones. Such is the case with the paradoxical figure of disembodied charity so heavy with love that it becomes incarnate – an image which is informed with the standard interpretation of Is. xiv, 8 and of the dew on the fleece of Gedeon.

In conclusion, it may be asked what general contribution this study has made to our knowledge and appreciation of *Piers Plowman* as a whole. In reply, it might be said that Langland's traditional imagery of charity has been placed in its dominant context, that the poetry itself has been re-examined and interpreted in the light of the traditional nature of its imagery, and that whenever the latter process has succeeded, a revitalization of the imagery has ensued. Second, the understanding and appreciation of poetry does not result from translating figurative into literal language; rather, the understanding and appreciation of poetry results from increasing and enhancing the reader's ability to comprehend the language of metaphor. In the case of traditional imagery, this end is best served, I think, by a study such as the foregoing. Third, though we can never transmute ourselves into the informed medieval reader of Langland, it is our responsibility to bring to the poem as much of the ideal response of such a reader as we are capable of. Fourth, the study has illumined an important characteristic of Langland's method of composition: it shows that his imagery is neither spontaneous outpouring nor rhetorical decoration; rather, it is evocative, logically and rationally constructed, and essential to the meaning of the poem. Finally, the study demonstrates the richness and complexity of the traditional connotations attached to Langland's imagery, and it exemplifies the amount of explanation often required by one or a few lines. In this regard, it is hoped that in its approach and method it may provide a kind of model for further intensive studies of this kind.

BIBLIOGRAPHY

1. TEXTS AND TRANSLATIONS OF PIERS PLOWMAN

Langland, William, *Piers Plowman: The A Version*, edited by George Kane (London, The Athlone Press, 1960).
——, *Piers the Ploughman*, translated by J. F. Goodridge (Baltimore, Penguin Books Inc., 1959).
——, *The Vision of William Concerning Piers the Plowman, In Three Parallel Texts Together With Richard the Redeless, by William Langland*, edited by Walter W. Skeat (Oxford, The Clarendon Press, 1886).
——, *Visions from Piers Plowman, Taken from the Poem of William Langland*, translated by Nevill Coghill (London, Phoenix House, 1953).

2. PRIMARY SOURCES

Biblia Sacra Vulgatae Editiones (Paris, 1838).
St. Bonaventura, *Collationes in Hexaemeron*, edited by Fr. Ferdinandus Delorme (Florence, Quaracchi, 1934).
——, *Opera Omnia*, 10 vols. (Florence, Quaracchi, 1882-1902).
Breviarium ad usum insignis Ecclesiae Sarum, edited by Francis Proctor and Christopher Wordsworth, 2 vols. (Cambridge, The University Press, 1882-1886).
Caxton, William, *The Royal Book* (Westminster, 1484).
Conrad of Hirshau, *Speculum Virginum*, B. M. Arundel 44, Date and provenance unknown.
Cornelius à Lapide, *Commentarii in Scripturam Sacram*, 10 vols. (Paris, 1875).
Denis the Carthusian, *Opera Omnia*, 42 vols. (Montreuil, 1896-1913), Vols. I-XIV.
Duns Scotus (?), *Grammaticae Speculativae* (Florence, Quaracchi, 1902).
Herrade de Landsberg, *Hortus Deliciarum*, Oberlin facsimile edition (Strassburg, 1945).
Holy Bible, The Douay-Rheims Version (Baltimore, The John Murphy Co., 1914).

104 BIBLIOGRAPHY

Hugh of St. Cher, *Opera Omnia in universum Vetus et Novum Testamentum*, 8 vols. (Venice, 1732).

John of Hoveden, *Philomena*, edited by Clemens Blume (Leipzig, O. R. Reisland, 1930).

Brother Laurent, "Sommes des Vices et des Vertus", edited by Ann Brooks Tysor, Unpublished M.A. thesis, University of North Carolina (1949).

Lydgate, John (?), *The Book of the Pilgrimage of the Soul* (Westminster, 1483).

Migne, J. P., *Patrologiae Cursus Completus Series Latina*, 220 vols. (Paris, 1884-1866).

Nicolas de Byard, *Dictionarius Pauperum* (Strassburg, 1516).

Nicolaus de Lyra, *Moralia super totam Bibliam* (Mantua, 1481).

——, *Postilla super totam Bibliam* (Venice, 1488).

Petrus Berchorius, *Liber Bibliae Moralis* (Cologne, 1477).

Pitra, J. B., *Spicilegium Solesmense*, 4 vols. (Paris, 1852-1858).

The Sarum Missale. Edited by J. Wickham Legg (Oxford, The Clarendon Press, 1916).

Speculum Humanae Salvationis, Facsimile edition by J. Ph. Berjeau (London, 1861).

Thomas of Erfurt (?), *Grammatica Speculativa*, translation by Charles Glenn Wallis of same work attributed above to Duns Scotus (Ann Arbor, Edwards Brothers, Inc., 1938).

Vincent de Beauvais, *Speculum Historiale* (Venice, 1494).

3. SECONDARY SOURCES

Bloomfield, Morton W., "Piers Plowman and the Three Grades of Chastity", *Anglia*, XLLVI (1958), pp. 227-253.

Boeckler, Albert, *Die Regensburg-Prüfeninger Buchmalerei des XII. und XIII. Jahrhunderts* (Munich, 1924).

Bradley, Henry, "Some Cruces in *Piers Plowman*", *Modern Language Review*, V (1910), pp. 340-342.

Burdach, Konrad, *Der Dichter des Ackermann aus Böhmen und seine Zeit, mit einer Einführung in das Gesamtwerk "Vom Mittelalter zur Reformation"*, 2 parts (Berlin, Weidmann, 1926, 1932).

Cayré, Fulbert, *Manual of Patrology and History of Theology*, 2 vols. Translated by H. Howitt (Paris, Desclée and Co., 1936, 1940).

Day, Mabel, "Duns Scotus and 'Piers Plowman' ", *Review of English Studies*, III (1927), pp. 333-334.

Dodwell, Charles Reginald, *The Canterbury School of Illumination 1066-1200* (Cambridge, The University Press, 1954).

Donaldson, E. Talbot, "Patristic Exegesis: The Opposition", *Critical Approaches to Medieval Literature. Selected Papers from the English Institute, 1958-1959*, edited by Dorothy Bethurum, pp. 27-60.

——, *Piers Plowman: The C-text and Its Poet* (= *Yale Studies in English*, Vol. 113) (New Haven, Yale University Press, 1949).

Donna, Sister Rose Bernard, *Despair and Hope: A Study in Langland and Augustine* (Washington, D.C., The Catholic University of America dissertation, 1948).

Dunning, Fr. T. P., *Piers Plowman: An Interpretation of the A-text* (New York, Longmans, Green and Co., 1937).

Encyclopedia of Religion and Ethics, 13 vols. Edited by James Hastings and others (New York, Charles Scribner's Sons, 1910-1927).

Erzgräber, Willi, *William Langlands Piers Plowman* (Heidelberg, The University Press, 1957).

Glorieux, Mgr. P., "Pour Revaloriser Migne", *Mélanges de Science Religieuse, Cahier Supplémentaire* (September 1952).

Greenhill, Eleanor Simmons, "The Child in the Tree: A Study of the Cosmological Tree in Christian Tradition", *Traditio*, X (1954), pp. 323-371.

Harrison, Frederick, *Treasures of Illumination: English Manuscripts of the Fourteenth Century* (London, The Studio, 1937).

Hirn, Yrjö, *The Sacred Shrine* (London, Macmillan and Co., 1912).

Hort, Greta, *Piers Plowman and Contemporary Religious Thought* (New York, The Macmillan Co., 1938).

Kaske, Robert E., "Eve's 'Leaps' in the *Ancrene Riwle*", *Medium Aevum*, XXIX (1960), pp. 22-24.

——, "Gigas the Giant in Piers Plowman", *Journal of English and Germanic Philology*, LVI (1957), pp. 177-185.

——, "Patristic Exegesis: The Defense", *Critical Approaches to Medieval Literature. Selected Papers from the English Institute, 1958-1959*. Edited by Dorothy Bethurum, pp. 27-60.

——, "The Speech of 'Book' in Piers Plowman", *Anglia*, LXXVII (1959), pp. 117-144.

Katzenellenbogen, Adolf, *Allegories of the Virtues and Vices in Medieval Art*, translated by Alan J. P. Crick (London, The Warburg Institute, 1939).

Knowlton, E. C., "Nature in Middle English", *Journal of English and Germanic Philology*, XX (1921), pp. 186-207.

Leidinger, Georg, *Meisterwerke der Buchmalerei* (Munich, Hugo Schmidt, 1920).

——, *Miniaturen aus Handschriften der Bayerischen Staatsbibliothek in München*, 4 vols. (Munich, Riehm and Tietze, 1912), Vol. IV.

de Lubac, Henri, *Exégèse médiévale: Les quatres sens de l'Ecriture* (Paris, Aubier, 1959).

Mâle, Émile, *L'Art Religieux de la Fin du Moyen Âge en France* (Paris, A. Colin, 1925).

——, *L'Art Religieux du XIIe Siècle en France* (Paris, A. Colin, 1924).

——, *L'Art Religieux du XIIIe Siècle en France*. Translated by Dora Nussey (London, J. M. Dent, 1913).

The New Schaff-Herzog Encyclopedia of Religious Knowledge, 12 vols. Edited by Samuel Macauley Jackson and others (New York, Funk and Wagnalls Co., 1908-1912).

Owen, Dorothy L., *Piers Plowman: A Comparison with Some Earlier and Contemporary French Allegories* (London, Hodder and Stroughton, 1912).

Raby, F. J. E., *A History of Christian-Latin Poetry from the Beginnings to the Close of the Middle Ages* (Oxford, The Clarendon Press, 1927).

Robertson, D. W., Jr., "The Doctrine of Charity in Medieval Literary Gardens: A Topical Approach through Symbolism and Allegory", *Speculum*, XXVI (1951), pp. 24-49.

——, "Historical Criticism", *English Institute Essays, 1950,* edited by Alan S. Downer, pp. 3-31.

——, and Huppé, B. F., *Piers Plowman and Scriptural Tradition* (Princeton, The University Press, 1951).

Smalley, Beryl, *The Study of the Bible in the Middle Ages* (Oxford, Blackwell's, 1952).

Spicq, Fr. C., *Esquisse d'une histoire de l'exégèse latine au Moyen Âge* (Paris, J. Vrin, 1944).

Tondelli, Leone, Reeves, Marjorie, and Hirsch-Reich, Beatrice, *Il Libro delle Figure dell'Abate Gioachimo da Fiore,* 2 vols. Second edition, revised (Turin, Società Editrice Internazionale, 1953), Vol. II.

Underwood, Paul A., "The Fountain of Life in Manuscripts of the Gospels", *Dumbarton Oaks Papers,* V (1950), pp. 43-138.

Watson, Arthur, *The Early Iconography of the Tree of Jesse* (London, H. Milford, 1934).

——, "The *Speculum Virginum* with Special Reference to the Tree of Jesse", *Speculum,* III (1928), pp. 445-469.

STUDIES IN ENGLISH LITERATURE

1. WILLIAM H. MATCHETT: *The Phoenix and the Turtle: Shakespeare's Poem and Chester's Loues Martyr.* 1965. 213 pp. Cloth.   Gld. 26.—

2. RONALD DAVID EMMA: *Milton's Grammar.* 1964. 164 pp.   Gld. 18.—

3. GEORGE A. PANICHAS: *Adventure in Consciousness: The Meaning of D. H. Lawrence's Religious Quest.* 1964. 225 pp., portrait.   Gld. 25.—

4. HENRIETTA TEN HARMSEL: *Jane Austen: A Study in Fictional Conventions.* 1964. 206 pp.   Gld. 25.—

5. DOROTHY SCHUCHMAN MCCOY: *Tradition and Convention: A Study of Periphrasis in English Pastoral Poetry from 1556-1715.* 1965. 289 pp.   Gld. 30.—

6. TED E. BOYLE: *Symbol and Meaning in the Fiction of Joseph Conrad.* 1965. 245 pp.   Gld. 24.—

7. JOSEPHINE O'BRIEN SCHAEFER: *The Three-Fold Nature of Reality of the Novels of Virginia Woolf.* 1965. 210 pp.   Gld. 24.—

8. GERARD ANTHONY PILECKI: *Shaw's "Geneva": A Critical Study of the Evolution of the Text in Relation to Shaw's Political Thought and Dramatic Practice.* 1965. 189 pp.   Gld. 20.—

9. BLAZE ODELL BONAZZA: *Shakespeare's Early Comedies: A Structural Analysis.* 1966. 125 pp. Cloth.   Gld. 18.—

10. THOMAS KRANIDAS: *The Fierce Equation: A Study of Milton's Decorum.* 1965. 165 pp. Cloth.   Gld. 21.—

11. KENNETH HUGH BYRON: *The Pessimism of James Thomson (B.V.) in Relation to his Times.* 1965. 174 pp. Cloth.   Gld. 20.—

12. ROLAND A. DUERKSEN: *Shelleyan Ideas in Victorian Literature.* 1966. 208 pp. Cloth.   Gld. 24.—

16. BARBARA BARTHOLOMEW: *Fortuna and Natura: A Reading of Three Chaucer Narratives.* 1966. 112 pp. Cloth. Gld. 17.—

18. EDWARD VASTA: *The Spiritual Basis of "Piers Plowman".* 1965. 143 pp. Cloth. Gld. 18.—

19. WILLIAM B. TOOLE: *Shakespeare's Problem Plays: Studies in Form and Meaning.* 1966. 242 pp. Cloth. Gld. 28.—

MOUTON & CO. — PUBLISHERS — THE HAGUE